# PLUCKLEY WAS MY PLAYGROUND

## 1919-1926

### FREDERICK SANDERS

CANTERLEY
PUBLISHING

*Pluckley was my playground*

Published by Canterley Publishing
www.canterley.co.uk
info@canterley.co.uk

Printed in the United Kingdom.

ISBN-13: 978-1-9164981-5-0

First published 2020.

# PLUCKLEY WAS MY PLAYGROUND
# 1919-1926

## FREDERICK SANDERS

*Dedicated to Lord Cornwallis, Lord Lieutenant of Kent.*

*The noble son of a great county who, by word and deed, has always helped
to hold fast all those things so dear to the hearts and minds
of all true Kentish men.*

*My mind lets go a thousand things,*
*Like dates of wars and deaths of kings,*
*And yet recalls the very hour —*
*'Twas noon by yonder village tower,*
*And on that last blue moon in May —*
*The wind came briskly up this way,*
*Crisping the brook beside the road;*
*Then, pausing here, set down its load*
*Of pine-scents, and shook listlessly*
*Two petals from that wild-rose tree.*

'Memory', by Thomas Bailey Aldrich

# FOREWORD

The period of time covered by this narrative is from September 1919 up to April 1926, when I was resident at Pluckley and the hamlet of Mundy Bois, the latter place being of the parish of Little Chart, though separated from the present parish by Pluckley and Egerton parishes.

I was born at Thorne Cottage, Pluckley Thorne, Pluckley, on 9th August 1908, and was away from my birthplace for most of the time up to September 1919.

At Pluckley Thorne is situated the public-house known as The Blacksmith's Arms, to which was attached a smith and a small grocer's shop. Next door to The Blacksmith's Arms was a large cottage, the home of the old road-foreman by the name of Mr 'Bonker' Woodcock. By his house was a smaller cottage, which many, many years before had been a butcher's shop and slaughterhouse, owned by well-known character Mr 'Puddeney' Weeks. This old butcher's business later became a boot and shoe repairer's premises taken over by Bonker's crippled son. Next to this came two very small farm-workers' cottages, in the first of which – the one adjoining the boot repairer's shop – I first saw the light of day. In the second cottage, the last one of this row, lived my great-uncle Ted Pile.

So at last, towards the end of 1919, I came home to my birthplace. It is of the following few years I write: of my schoolboy friends and our adventures, and of the many and varied people in and around my village of those years. This is a true chronicle simply told, of real people and places. As far as I can trace there have been Piles in

Pluckley parish, and it is no doubt that my love for my birthplace has been made so much stronger on account of the varied accumulations of inbred feelings; an instinctive awareness, sub-consciously recognising this particular parish as the habitat and environment of those former generations of my mother's forebears, reaching back into much older times.

The late Mr Henry E. Turff, who was headmaster at Pluckley School from 1901 to 1929 (when he retired), once told me that in an old school attendance register he had unearthed – after he had taken over from a former headmaster by the name of Mr Coe to whom the villagers had given the nickname of 'Mad Coe' – that he found at one time nearly all the children attending the school over a long period consisted almost solely of Piles and Skinners (both old-standing families and their branches) in about equal proportions. There were a few other odd families. My own parents were married at Pluckley Church (St Nicholas's) on 18th September 1907: Sergeant Frederick William Sanders of the Army Pay Corps, and Alice Pile. On their wedding day the Rev. W.D. Springett DD (who later became the Rev. Canon Springett DD) in a short address in the church mentioned that just a hundred years before, a Miss Pile of Pluckley had been married to a Sergeant Houghton of the 25th Light Dragoons. Houghton is another very old Pluckley family.

As adventures and natural history cannot be confined to just one particular parish where Kentish schoolboys are concerned, it needs mention of things of interest and of other people in the villages around, and so we have such nearby parishes as Egerton, Little Chart, Hothfield, Smarden and Charing getting into the picture from time to time to help make an even better chronicle and to give a wider scope to this work.

This tale is not being written in strict chronological order: for memory is at times a fickle jade! There are many short and longer examples of exact periods of time covering many parts of this narrative, and there are many incidents which occurred to which no set dates can be given, only that they happened in some particular year, either in the spring, summer, autumn or winter seasons. This is a story that is told – as round a camp-fire, or around the hearth in one's home, or upon some sunny, grassy hillside – moving in conversation from one thing to another, each point forming a fresh piece of kaleidoscopic picturing, to gradually build up the greater pattern, that upon completion will finally form a full picture of hundreds of facts... the chronicle, over a number of years, of the village of Pluckley, and its near neighbours.

Most of the notes relative to this book were made in 1927; further notes being added in 1931. After writing *Kentish Wealden Dialect* in 1935, *Kentish Weald Churchyards* in 1936 and *The Natural History of Mundy Bois* in 1936-7, I intended to begin this Pluckley Chronicle in 1937. The end of 1937 saw the beginning of *Lawrence of Arabia: a psychological analysis of a Man of Destiny* which I completed in 1938. Again this narrative came under review only to be deferred when I began in 1938 my scientific investigation into Kentish ghost-lore and legend. Then came World War II and a period of three years in the Royal Artillery. Back home again I settled down to write *Psychical Research in Haunted Kent* and followed this up with another dialect book in *The Dialect of Kent*. The ghost-legend investigation continued, in between which were sandwiched five expedition to Deadman's Island, and later the *Flying Saucers over Kent* investigation. Short stories and novelettes upon the weird and the macabre for British and American papers and magazines followed, until now, at long last, after all these years of putting off the writing of the Pluckley Chronicles, I find myself upon a clearer sea of literary effort.

So this evening of the 16th April 1955, I have really made a start upon those long-deferred notes penned firstly twenty-eight years ago to begin this, the BOOK OF MY HEART.

Frederick W.T. Sanders
42 Sydney Road
Chatham

10th December 1956: it is nearly two years since I began this work and now it is finished. Before I ever began to pen the Pluckley Chronicles, many of the people mentioned in them had passed away, including my old schoolboy chum John Beale. Yet here in this book they live again, and because of this I am happy. This is a narration of those who lived and died, and of those who still live on.

Their names endureth and their habitations shall not be lost.

Frederick W.T. Sanders
Chatham

10th December 1956

# PUBLISHER'S NOTE

On completion of *Pluckley was my playground* in December 1956, a very few carbon-typed and bound copies were produced by Frederick Sanders to be given to family members and deposited in public libraries.

The text that follows is taken from this first typescript; though with a few minor edits to clarify certain points, remove obvious mistakes and excessive repetition, and to honour the author's own desire to censor, in retrospect, one or two points that might have been seen to be injurious to those described.

Much of Pluckley's surroundings have changed in the century since the events herein described. Park Wood, the Shave and much of Wonder Wood have long since been scrubbed out, and there is no longer a trace of such features as Pluckley Mill, Garden Pond or the Haunted Laurels. Nonetheless, plenty is still recognisable from Sanders' text, such as the village centre, the trees of Three Oaks Meadow, the Pinnock Stream and many of his beloved fields and ponds. Thanks to a good network of public rights-of-way in the area – to which Sanders himself alludes – readers may enjoy tracing his footsteps and seeing what remains for themselves.

*Every adventure must begin*
*somewhere, just as every*
*adventure must end somewhere, too!*

*When the swallow comes again*, by Frederick Sanders

# CHAPTER ONE

Where then shall our quest for rural adventure, knowledge and humour begin? It shall start at the top of a little lane, the first turning on the left about mid-way up Pluckley Hill.

Dicky Buss's Lane shot off suddenly and steeply from the Pluckley Hill Road. On the right-hand side of the lane was a squarely-built cottage in which the Crouchers lived. Here dwelt William Croucher, known to us as 'Willie', and by some profound oversight on our part he never attained the honour of a nickname. He was just plain Willie. Up some stone steps to the left and upon an eminence stood the large, well-built home of Mr Turner, the village carpenter and builder, plumber and undertaker. 'Dapper' Turner had two sons and one daughter. His red-headed male offspring did not revel in the names bestowed upon them by their schoolchums, for the eldest was called 'Carrots' and the other 'Ginger'! Miss Turner was quiet, reserved and ladylike and smart in her way as her father was dapper in his. Mrs Turner, like the wives of other village tradesmen, was known to exist though rarely if ever seen. Mr Turner was, in his way, next to 'Gaffer' Turff, the village school headmaster, a leading villager beneath the high position of the rector, the Rev. Canon Springett DD, who occupied the second position in the parish below that of the exalted leadership of the squire, Sir Henry Dering, Baronet. He, like the tradesmen's wives, was known to exist – but in an exalted manner, of course! – though also being rarely encountered. Perhaps twice a year he would enter the private chapel of the Derings in the village church to set an example to his parishioners. Now and then he would patronise the Garden Fete held each summer in the beautiful grounds of the rectory, to lend prestige to this wonderful event, and to show that even he, the Lord of the Manor, the Baronet, the Squire, feudal keeper of the lands of Pluckley, was great enough to hobnob with his modern-day serfs... at a distance of approximately twenty yards!

But even for all his possessions and ancient lineage he did not count perhaps so much as did the rector and Dapper Turner, Doctor Littledale (who lived at Charing three miles away and who had a surgery in the village) and Jacob Miles the sexton. Through the capable hands of these men the villagers passed at some time or another for something or other: to be born or married; baptised or cured; to be 'boxed' and buried. To us schoolboys it was Old Jacob ('Mister Miles to you, my boy!' my grandmother would admonish me) who was the king-pin of this wonderful and awesome quartet. For did not Old Jacob wear a marvellous collar, though never a tie with it, which was made of celluloid and could be bathed, dried and cleaned by the simple expedient of spitting upon a large red handkercher with white spots on it? And stamped upon this collar he always wore was a rule of so many inches, marked in halves, quarters and eighths-of-an-inch. With this he would measure the girth of a tree or the spacing for rows of vegetables on his allotment; or fix the exact spacing and depth of a grave upon which he might be called to plot off and excavate in his important role as the sexton of the church. The collar of Old Jacob set an awful finality to things mortal, just as did the doctor's awesome remark on one occasion when he said that 'When you are dead, you *are* dead!'

Now where are we? Ah! for sure, at the beginning of our adventures and Dicky Buss's Lane, which shot off suddenly and ran away steeply from the old hill road. A little way down the lane, on the left, was situated a small field, part of the land of the old miller Richard Buss, whose home was adown Pluckley Hill, opposite the old black and white thatched house of Mr Wood the village blacksmith. These two men we held in awe to a great extent that they held us enthralled by their very interesting and important occupations. This field of the miller's became known as the Blue Field to us, for in the summer the Germander Speedwell would appear almost overnight and blossom forth into millions of sky-blue flowers so that the pasture became covered as with a quilt cut from out the summer sky. These exquisite tiny blooms were called by us either 'Birds' Eyes' or Cats' Eyes' and at times by the appellation of 'The Little Blue Flowers'. It was in this place we often played during school-time break from 12 o'clock until 1.30: mostly in the spring, when the birds were nesting and beginning their clutches of eggs.

The chief of the two games reserved for this playing-spot was one called 'Birds', the other being 'Foxes and Rabbits'. The former game was the popular one but when we got tired of it then it degenerated into the rollicking and un-educational play of the latter. Usually about a dozen of the younger lads would repair to the Blue Field, each to become a bird and build a nest, lay eggs and fly, sing and call according to whichever feathered avian's cloak of feathers we flew under. Many of us made some imitation of birds' songs and calls. How we would fly, flapping our arms as we ran about, gathering nesting materials, imitating the very flight of the birds. Here a 'blackbird' would whistle or sound it harsh warning-call; an 'owl' would hoot or scream; a common 'rook' would caw or a 'jay' chatter and scold! Stones and pebbles were usually secured for eggs, though 'Rusty' Blackman (who lived near to Mrs Jennings' sweetshop) once used the small marble-like black droppings of a sheep to represent the tiny eggs of a long-tailed tit he was impersonating, which lovely small bird has been known to lay anything up to a dozen eggs in the feathered interior of its lichen-covered oval nest. Now and again someone would be a 'golden eagle' (though I'm afraid there wasn't one within 200 miles' radius of Pluckley – other than in captivity in a zoo). As no-one seemed to know what sort of noise an eagle made the impersonator would cry out a loud and harsh 'KRAA-ARK!!' Once an 'albatross' came to life and flew around upon motionless wings in ever-widening circles, uttering no call, making no nest or even laying an egg, until it collided with a 'Jenny wren', which immediately lost its short temper and set about the poor albatross in no uncertain manner. When, eventually, we tired of this game 'Foxes and Rabbits' was given a session. The lower part of the field was the warren, and one of the lads would be a fox. The rabbits had to come out of the warren and nip about, it being the duty of the fox to catch one of them, whereupon the one getting captured became a fox also, and so the game went on until all or nearly all the rabbits were caught, and had become foxes.

******

At the 'end' of Dicky Buss's Lane, which really and truly was not the actual end of this rough – at one time – private road to Pluckley Hill, upon which one side of the Blue Field abutted, is a pond, also called after the name of Richard Buss the miller, as Dicky Buss's Pond. In the long-ago it had been a cattle and horse-pond and used by bygone millions as a means for swelling up the spokes and rims of the wheels of their carts and wagons in dry weather. The vehicle was run into the centre of the pond and the wheels left to soak up water and so swell as to tighten up the spokes in the woodwork of the hubs and rims.

In this piece of high upland water lived hundreds of common smooth newts, known to zoology as *Triton vulgaris*, and to Pluckley schoolboys in their own idiom as 'effets'. The patriarchs of the village called them 'poison lizards', the former word of the two pronounced 'pizen' in the Kent dialect. It was at this pond, in the spring of 1920, a few months after coming home to Pluckley at the age of eleven years, that I became known as the Wizard, and in the following years as the Naturalist-who-is-a-Wizard. How it came about was once the matter of these smooth newts, held in awe and horror by old and young alike in the parish. As most of my eleven years had been spent in military barracks in or near big towns and cities, and in semi-regimented private houses in such towns as Woolwich and cities as Dublin, my young mind had accumulated vast stores of knowledge giving a very much broader outlook to life shed of native superstitions. Everything about me, at Pluckley, was mostly new and wonderful: a vast potential of learning and exploration. So that spring afternoon, when I had first noted the little brownish creatures immobile upon the mud at the pond's bottom, I had the urge to catch some, handle and inspect them.

When it became apparent to my playmates of that particular time that I was trying to capture these lizard-like amphibians, they cried out in great alarm for me to desist. They said, quite fearfully, that I should be poisoned if I even touch one, and that I would die if stung by one. Yet I persisted in my solitary efforts. At the side of me and a little way off stood Willie Croucher and his sister, and Rusty Blackman and his sister, huddled together and fearful for me. Then, slowly putting an arm down into the clear water, I spread out the fingers of the hand over the motionless newt. A swift downwards, slightly forward movement and I withdrew my arm, in the hand of which I clutched dribbling black mud and a pizen lizard!

Willie and Rusty and the two girls gazed at me with apprehension in their eyes. I washed the mud from my hand and placed the beautifully smooth little creature, with its gem-like eyes, upon the palm of my hand, and then opened its jaws to show that no sting was within its mouth. Yet they were unconvinced and, avoiding me, hurried away up the lane back to the village to spread the dread news that young Fred

Sanders was as good as dead. That was on the Saturday. When I arrived at school on the Monday I was met with many astonished faces... for it seemed to my schoolmates that I had indeed returned from the dead. Yet that happening convinced them I had supernatural powers. Later I added other powers to my reputation by breaking off blackthorn twigs to show that they could not give me convulsions ending with a painful demise. I took an egg from a robin's nest, for my collection, and did not get my eyes pecked out for my temerity. I wore the white blossoms of the maythorn pinned to my blue jersey and nothing awkward happened to me, though my grandmother, old Mrs Jesse Pile, called me a 'daring naughty boy' and my mother severely scolded me, for the folklore of old Pluckley was etched deep within her. I captured grass snakes and the silvery scaled legless lizards called slow-worms, and continued to survive. When I put my fingers in the nests of the Jenny wrens my digits never withered and fell off, and no disaster overtook me when I would not spit upon the toe-cap of my right boot and mark the spittle with a cross, after seeming my first piebald horse one day, upon the road to Charing.

\*\*\*\*\*\*

Just above the pond of the old and bearded miller, upon a slope grew several great trees, known to the village as 'The Laurels', though these fine trees were bay-laurels, and evidently in the long-ago had been planted there for picturesque effect by order of, no doubt, old Sir Edward Dering who had been the father of Sir Henry. To these great and gloomy evergreens a terrible happening clung. They became known, in the year 1919, as the 'Haunted Laurels', on account of a schoolmaster of Smarden having committed suicide by hanging himself in that darksome grove. He was missing for several weeks, until one evening, old Richard Buss happened to go through The Laurels and was 'kicked' in the face by the suspended thing that had once been a man.

The birds had long pecked out his eyes, and rats had eaten away his lips, tongue, nose and ears. This awful effigy seemed alive, as it wreathed about beneath its stained clothing, for the flesh was a mass of rolling white maggots. And a great quantity of them had cascaded down upon the hapless head and face of the old miller as he bumped into the booted feet of the dead master. No-one knew why the master from Smarden killed himself. Mr Turff, our own headmaster, told us lads that this schoolmaster had often walked the three miles from Smarden to Pluckley to partake of refreshment in the private bar of the main village hostelry in Pluckley Street, the Black Horse, and to discourse upon logic with him. Logical he may have been in life, yet no logic could explain away his suicide.

Yet the Haunted Laurels held no terrors for us schoolboys in daylight and they became one of our favourite playing places. These high trees, throwing afar their smooth boughs, were smothered all over with 'Old Man's Beard', the Traveller, a joy of the botanists. We would climb up and down their heights by way of the tough creepers, which later I called 'lianas'. Then one day a wonderful book came into my hands, brought home by my father on one of his infrequent leaves from the Royal Air Force to which he belonged in those days. This was the novel by Edgar Rice Burroughs, *Tarzan of the Apes*. After assimilating this book a new game came into being in the Haunted Laurels called 'Tarzans' which consisted mainly in swinging from bough to bough, tree to tree upon the sawing liana' of the Old Man's Beard and the peaceful air was filled with blood-curdling cries as we thumped with our fists upon our chests… either as 'Tarzans' or as 'Apes'. The smaller tendrils of the 'Traveller's Joy' we called 'Smoking Cane', and the old dried out ones we would cut up into 'cigarettes' and smoke them with much relish until the acrid, biting smoke made our tongues sore and we had to leave off for a time until this unpleasant effect had worn off.

******

As mentioned previously the old lane did not end at the pond, but continued up to the Great Barn and its outhouses and cowsheds upon the slopes of Park Wood Meadow. Then it turned right and round up and along the brink of one of the sweeping slopes of Pluckley Hill, where stood Pluckley Mill. From the mill it continued on until it came out opposite Kingsland Cottages on the Pluckley to Egerton road. The barn, outhouses and cowsheds also belonged to Miller Buss and, of course, the barn had to be 'Dicky Buss's Barn'.

It was a large structure of ragstone and timber with a tiled roof. This place was the scene of numerous adventures and escapades of which more will be told further on in this narrative. It was not far from the Great Barn to the Haunted Laurels and it was while playing one day around the barn and the old buildings that my two bosom chums John and Robert Beale, whose father farmed at Pebbles Hill away off in the near distance, suddenly remembered that they had a 'great secret' to impart to me. It was over near the Laurels, they explained. Bob had made the discovery and let his brother into the secret, and I am now about to share it, too. Upon a flat part of the bank above the Lizard Pond we stopped, and Bob pulled away thin turfs of grass to reveal a trap-door, about three feet square, made of oak-wood and blackened with age. We prised it open and swung it back flat upon its creaking hinges and I saw below a great, gaping dark place. I lay down flat and looked down into the depths, but could see little until my eyes had become accustomed to the twilight below. It was a large underground cistern, with bricked sides, faced with cement. It was about ten feet deep and crystal-clear water lay in it three or four in height. This was evidently a spring-fed cavern as I could hear water tinkling somewhere to my left below. A small orifice in the wall on the right took the overflow and this ran down a pipe, well underground, and emptied itself into the Lizard Pond. But what amazed me was the amount of life imprisoned within this secret place. Several large smooth snakes, known as water snakes, were there, as well as numerous frogs and quite a cohort of newts. Snails crawled or clung upon the walls, while many pond-side insects flew about in the gloom. How had they come there, all these creatures? No doubt by crawling up the waste-water pipe just above the pond when they were very, very small, and when the overflow was not in action. Once in the underground place they lost their way, and, feeding each upon each as to its kind, grew and if, by some fortunate chance they eventually found the road to escape, they found it blocked by their increased size and girth. Yes, it was a wonderful place and a grand secret.

******

Just wide of the Great Barn was a little hut on wheels with an iron chimney sticking up from its roof. This was the home of 'Dusty' Buss, the old miller's son who had lived a wandering life in his younger days and have even consorted with those wanderers of the Kentish Weald, the gipsies. He had never done any regular work, and was the despair of his hard-working, god-fearing parent. Much of Dusty's time was put in, in and around the Black Horse. Then he did odd-job work for Mr Fidler, the licensee, by driving the village horse and cart to and from Pluckley Station, about a mile south of the village. He would attend weddings and funerals and also with the light-van horse and van would move people from place to place with their families and chattels. He knew every place of refreshment upon the roads for twenty miles around and he always advised a 'nip for the road' at starting and a 'nip for the road' halfway and one for the journey's end. And of course, if folks being moved had one, then of course, it was only common decency to treat the thirst-throated Dusty as well! He loved the wild songster birds, as well as others, but only on account of their marketable value. He would trap chaffinches, goldfinches, thrushes and blackbirds, and keep them well-fed and looked after until they got over their captivity and sang and sang again. These he sold to people who wanted a singing bird. He also caught owls and tamed them for those who wished to have them in their homes or outhouses for catching mice, at which they were even more proficient than the lean, hungry and specially-bred farm cats. Or he would get you a young jay or a magpie, or a jackdaw. Thus lived Dusty Buss, the wanderer, the village bird-trapper and trainer.

******

It was in the old rambling barn, with its boarded-off section for stables, coaches, chaff-cutter and stores, and the hay-loft and the great upper storage room for corn, oats and barley, that I found the wild black kitten. It was Willie Croucher who told me about the nest of wild kittens in the stable of the barn. 'Somebody keeps catching one every day or so,' he remarked, 'and drowning them in the Roach Pond back of the barn!' I was puzzled over this, so I asked him why the unknown person had not drowned all the kittens at the same time. 'Because they clear out of their nest and scatter all over the barn' was Willie's explanation.

He told me there had been six but three had been drowned for he had found their pathetic little bodies floating amongst the duck-weed of the pond. 'Two last week and one yesterday,' he explained. Of the three left there was one black kitten and two tabbies. So after school one day Willie and I went down to the barn. Tiptoeing in I saw the nest of hay in the corner and the three kittens. 'I'm going to catch the black one,' I whispered, 'and keep him!' As the kittens opened their eyes and made ready to spring off I dived and caught the gleaming-eyed black kitten already spitting, biting and scratching. I rolled the lower front portion of my blue jersey over and over him, and set off home with it scrabbling and mewing in anger within the folds. Willie called out after me 'You'll never keep it! Dusty Buss says you can't tame wild 'uns, they either escape or just die on you!' When I arrived home the kitten was put down on the floor by the fireside where a saucer of milk had been placed by my mother. It went straight to the milk and lapped it all up and cleared away several pieces of cooked dried herring. I sat down in my chair and the black kitten climbed up my leg and settled itself upon my lap and purring happily went to sleep.

The wild kitten was tamed! I called him 'Questie' after the black-cat mascot of Sir Ernest Shackleton's ship *Quest* which sailed for the Antarctic that year – 1921 – and upon which Sir Ernest died on January 5th the following year.

The day following the capture of Questie, Willie Croucher informed me that he had been down to the barn early that morning and that the nest was empty. The other two kittens floated dead in the little round fish pond. The killer of the kittens was never brought to light, through Willie and the Beales and myself thought it may have been Dusty Buss, on account of the safety of his captured birds he kept in his hut home. So we got a piece of chalk and inscribed upon the door of the hut in large white letters, KITTEN MURDERER, and left it at that.

******

The small round piece of water between the great barn and its outbuildings, and the old-fashioned cowshed (a real relic of other days, for it was built of wide flat boards, had a very thick thatched roof and the front was entirely open) had previously always been called Barn

Pond. Then, in 1921, the year of the Great Drought, when the fields lay white beneath the flaming sun, and great fissures made a wild patterning over the cultivated and the grass lands, we found that fish inhabited this pond. Not just a few, but hundreds! They were roach, pretty and sporting fish.

As the water in this pond diminished so did the weaker fish die and one Saturday morning, that courier of near villages' news (Willie Croucher) came over to tell 'The Terrible Three' – Bob, John and myself, for by that collective title we had gradually become to be known – that 'thousands of fishes' were floating dead in the Barn Pond. So off we set, post-haste, from Prebbles Hill Farm, the home of Mr Beale, to the pond of the dead fishes. The sunlight was scorching down and the sound of numerous noisy insects permeated the dancing atmosphere, and there upon the surface of the pond denuded even of the ubiquitous duck-weed, floated the whitening corpses of scores of roach. In the six inches or so of water still remaining in the pond we could see shoals of live roach moving about. 'We want rain now to save 'em,' said Willie. Though there seemed little or no hope of that. 'We could take a lot of the live ones out and put them in other ponds,' I suggested. To which Bob replied: 'What other ponds?' So we had a tally up. Dicky Buss's Pond was dry and there were only two or three inches of water in the underground 'secret' cavern. Watercress Pond, Moorhen Pond, Honey Farm Pond, Wild Pond, Thorne Ruffits Pond, Bluehill Pond, and most of the other ponds were either dry or in a similar condition to that of Barn Pond. We let the matter drop and a few days afterwards this pond was nearly dry and most of the fish dead. Finally it dried up and all the remaining fish died. Yet it brought one change to the pond, for ever afterwards it was called Roach Pond instead of Barn Pond.

'Anyway,' said Willie, 'we can make a short cut now by climbing round the end of the old board fence.' This fence projected about a quarter the way across the pond, forming a boundary to stop cattle strays from the Mill Banks Field into the barns area. The pond had ebbed far from its original margins and upon the dried mud, once underwater, Willie walked to essay the 'short cut'. He got halfway round the end of the boarded fence, caught his grey jersey upon an old nail and while struggling to free himself, slipped and went backwards into the pond. The water went up in a muddy spout and Willie scrambled ashore, still on one side, covered with mud and smelling of strange and peculiar odours! How we laughed! But Willie took it all philosophically as we wiped off as much of the mud as we could with handfuls of dried grass. Then we saw Willie home, and stood grinning outside his garden gate as we listened to Mrs Croucher scolding her son, and lustily smacking him about his muddled head.

*And back among the lime tree leaves,*
*Grown gold before they fall,*
*I heard the song that autumn weaves*
*When first the wild winds call;*
*And though their hand is chill and cold,*
*Their face has winter's frown,*
*I know them for the friends of old*
*That shook the apples down.*

'The Apple Winds', by W.H. Ogilvie

# CHAPTER TWO

The south wall of Miller Buss's old barn abutted on the northern boundary of Park Wood Meadow, that swept down to meet the eastern side of Park Wood. How many times I galloped at full speed adown this lovely pasture I cannot be sure, but no doubt it would be near the thousand mark. It was here that I found my first autumn crocus, in all its leafless, flowering beauty. It was the only blossom ever discovered in this parish or in the parishes adjoining. Many a time my cousin, Jim Pile, and myself had searched for further specimens, but none ever came to light. Another of our chief searches was for the wild fitillery, or snake flower, and though we wandered all over the parish we never found a single bloom. The only oxslip ever recorded in Pluckley I found by accident, when bird-nesting in a field on Farmer Jesse Buss's land at Elvey Farm. I slipped off the top of a deep drainage ditch, landing up in the mud at the bottom, to find myself gazing at a flower I had never seen – an oxslip! This spring wild flower was added to the special 'search-list', but though Jim and I tramped miles looking for them we never found another. It is most peculiar how some flowers keep themselves so rare, yet what an adventure it is looking for them, and when found to give greater satisfaction to the young heart than all the gold in old California!

There was one other flower we never stumbled across and this was the wild foxglove. It could be found at nearby Hothfield, and out on Charing Heath, and in such profusion in the first woods back of the North Downs beyond Charing that the very number of them and the glorious colour held one spellbound. So spellbound, so awed, that I never even thought of picking any! It was beyond my very youthful comprehension, yet something stirring in my subconsciousness tried to tell me that here amidst these galaxies of flowers brooded the very spirit of the Creator of all things. In these foxglove woods of sweetly-scented firs God took on a new shape, became more comprehensible, and the God whom I had been taught to fear in church and at Sunday school, became instead someone to be *loved*! A wonderful great-father, teacher, confidante and gentle friend.

******

Park Wood itself was a game preserve for pheasants, the birds owned by Sir Henry of Surrenden Dering. This wood teamed with these game birds that were looked after, and fed on grain, and who would come to the gamekeeper's call and follow him about like so many farmyard fowls, trotting behind the friendly figure that gave them food and protection. Halfway through this wood was a crossroads, made up of the old stoney right-o'-way footpath and the long soft-surfaced road or drive which ran from north to south through Park Wood. Not far along the left-hand turning could be seen the gamekeeper's hut, on wheels, in which were kept so many things: food and medicines for the pheasants; gin-traps and wires to catch the enemies of the pheasants; wire, nails, binding-twine, hen-coops, and old coats, boots and sacks, with maybe a truss of sweet-smelling hay or a pale-gold bundle of wheat-straw.

Nearby the hut was the gamekeeper's gibbet upon which were hung his victims, the acknowledged malefactors of the wild folks in a game preserve… the robbers and the killers! There they would hang until their feathers and skins dropped away, and until cartilages and muscles rotted when the whitened skeletons would drop apart and litter the putrid earth below the gibbet. Here I have seen jays, and stoats, rooks and rats, grass snakes and butcher-birds, magpies and domestic cats swinging gently yet grotesquely, in the breeze, all lumped together as common felons. So it was in Sir Henry's time, and before in the time of his father the good Sir Edward and even beyond, generation upon generation back when other game was abroad in the shapes of preserved deer, when it was men who hung upon a stouter gibbet instead of foxes, cats and jay-birds. Men torn with round ball-shot; men mangled in man-traps; men transfixed by the long shafts of bowmen, whose bows were made from the yew-trees grown in the old churchyard on Pluckley Hill hard by the village street.

******

There was a ghost that haunted this wood: maybe it does still. It was our headmaster, Mr Turff, whom we affectionately called 'Old Gaffer', between ourselves, who told us the tale of the Colonel's ghost. His name had become forgotten, and also the reason why he hanged himself from the oak tree on the left-hand side of the lower half of the stoney pathway through the wood. As dusk (so the story goes) merges into the deeper gloom of night the spectre of the old colonel can be seen depending from the running-noose of the rope tightened around a main limb that projects over the path. Very few in Pluckley cared to wend their way through any kind of a wood, haunted or otherwise, after day, and about the only ones who ever traversed Park Wood after dark were myself and my two chums Bob and John Beale, whichever gamekeeper who might be on duty, and the second son of 'Old Go-dup' or Mr Goldup, of The Hollies, a stone's throw from the old square-sided inn The Rose and Crown near the borders of Mundy Bois. This younger 'Go-dup' who worked at the hand-making paper works of Mr Bachelor at Little Chart (the present parish of the isolated portion named Mundy Bois) never worried about the ghost, for he was usually, about eleven-thirty at night, so well fortified with 'convivial spirit' from the hostelry of the Swan in Little Chart village, at the end of Swan Lane, that he never gave such things as apparitions a second thought. I recall how I would gather speed down the stoney path after entering the wood around dusk in the summer, or after dark during winter-time, until I was going full belt like an express train as I passed the fatal oak tree in case the dreaded shade of the long-dead Colonel had, or might happen to, materialise. I took no chances: though no ghost would have kept me from going anywhere after dark, just as long as I could run: and in those days I could run, like a deer, for miles and never 'catch a stitch' and without a laboured puff even enough to blow out a candle's flame, as Tom Webster, the *Daily Mail* sports cartoonist said of Nurmi, the famous Finnish runner.

\*\*\*\*\*\*

Beyond the gateway at the end of the right-o'-way at the southern end of Park Wood was a very long piece of pasturage known as Jesse Buss's Field, part of the farmland of Elvey Farm owned by Mr J. Buss. In the year of the Great Drought of 1921, when mushrooms grew there as they had never grown before, in such extraordinary profusion that they actually turned the great meadow as white as snow with their umbrella-like tops, I changed the name of this pasture to Mushroom Meadow and so it remained. That mushrooming season we ate mushrooms until we began to look like those succulent edible fungi! We had them fried and we had them stewed and even made into jellies that did not look uncommonly like pigs'-head brawn that my mother and my grandmother (who lived over at Hawthorn Cottage on the Station Road, not far above the old Fir Toll at Pluckley) used to make so beautifully, deliciously stiff, and really meaty! Oh, those heavenly slices of brawn slapped in between thick slices of new bread still warm from the old bakery of another Mr Buss of Pluckley, who was the village baker in those days. It was in Mushroom Meadow where the rabbits from the southern confines of the haunted wood would gather to feed in the cool of summer evenings and now and again I have seen strange black wild-rabbits feeding with the ordinary brown wild-rabbits. This strange fact I mentioned to my grandfather Jesse Pile, known as 'Independence' Pile, on account of him being the most independent man in the parish of Pluckley. He said that these black rabbits, born of the common wild brown rabbits were 'throw-backs' in the line of descent from where at some time or another a tame black rabbit had escaped from its hutch in the village and wandered off and 'gone wild', breeding with the wild ones and so giving the predominant 'black strain' to the wild brown rabbit strain.

Beyond the Mushroom Meadow lay a small square field which was called Little Marsh Field, on account of it being flooded all over after prolonged heavy rains. Its surface was a trifle below the surrounding ground level and so it flooded easily. Originally a hop-garden, almost beyond living memory, it still retained the deep forms of the drainage furrows, though these had become very much smoothed away, though still very discernible. It was in this field, under one of the hedges, where I found my first partridge nest, full of shiny olive-coloured eggs. The next field on, known as Honey Farm Field, after the old farm situated near one corner of it, was one of those mysterious, exciting pieces of ground one happens upon from time-to-time. Much of the excitement came from the 'mad' dog, as we called it, that kept watch and ward over this isolated farmstead in which lived a family known as the Austins. Some were Austins, some Smiths, and one of the young Austin men went under the nicknames of 'Plushey' and one of the Smith youths as 'Doddie'. They had no explanation to offer for such names, and no-one seemed to know why they had been blessed with them. In front of the farm a large, rush-bordered pond could be seen in which vast numbers of 'effets' or newts lived and led none-too-placid existences; for this pond was the playground of the dozen or so ducks from Honey Farm, who were the most criss-crossed crew of ducks one ever did see and as wary a bunch of waddlers as ever were born. Over in one corner towards the outer farmlands of Mr Small of Pinnock Farm, was a sheet of deep water, out of which grew high rushes and bulrushes as well as quite tall trees with long gnarled branches like the distorted arms of skeletons seeking outwards as if to clutch at anything that came their way.

This ghostly old pond was cluttered up with the submerged branches of many generations of trees and bushes and below the duckweed-spattered surface they would clutch at the foolhardy explorer trying to reach the moorhens' nests cut among the reeds at its centre. The more the daring egg-collector struggled the more he became entangled, to be finally plunged into the water. Luck and the fear of death would make him crash and struggle, exhausted, to the grassy bank, where he would find, upon examining his bare feet and legs, nasty cuts and scratches, some of which he would carry as old scars all through life.

It was here that I discovered, high up in a tall thin tree which leaned out over the pond, a nest of sticks. Slowly I climbed up and up, and the tree leaned further and further out over the water, even beneath my youthful five stones of weight. As I neared the nest, a large bird detached itself with a terrific clatter of its beating wings. Frightened, I clung hard and cowered against the slender top of the trunk. But the large and beautiful bird − for it was a turtle-dove − flew away and disappeared through the trees on the other side of the pond. I reached the nest, and the tree-top sagged beneath my weight. Would it break and precipitate me into the deep water below with its horrible tangle of vicious old branches, tangled and lying in wait to receive my hurtling form? There would not have been much chance of surviving. Death by drowning was truly on the cards, held down by those shiny black water-logged arms of ancient branches, keepers of the life and peace of this fantastic spot! Then began the descent. But how was I to get the large white egg I intended adding to my collection down safely, as well as myself? The egg was rather large to carry successfully in my mouth, so clinging tight to the leaning, gentle swaying trunk of the tree, I contrived to pull up my jersey with my right hand in which the egg was held; bringing the bottom of the jersey up, I gritted it with my teeth and safely deposited in its fold the precious egg of the turtle-dove. Then slowly but surely, and gaining confidence at every foot gained downwards, I descended until I reached the ground and I could breathe freely once again.

In the bushes near this old pond the mistle-thrushes nested in large numbers. Their nests were similar to the blackbirds' though, like their eggs, dissimilar to those of the song thrush. There is nothing to vie in beauty, from all the varied coloured eggs of the wild birds, with the sky-blueness of the song thrush's eggs with their jet-black spots and markings. Gems of the wild, whose beauty one carries through life as a very delightful, heavenly memory.

******

But of the 'mad' dog of Honey Farm. This black and white watchdog, which seemed a mixture of collie sheepdog, black-retriever and water-spaniel, held we children as the absolute bane of its tied-up existence. He lived in a kennel in the garden of the farm, and in the days of spring and summer when we used the right-o'-way, or field-path, to take us on part of our way to school at Pluckley from the tiny hamlet of Mundy Bois, the 'Old Devil' as we called him would ramp and rage and tear about growling and barking in the uttermost ferocious manner. Time and time again his long chain, with its gleaming steel links, would pull him up short upon his haunches, or throw him sideways choking for air from the pressure of the stout leather collar around his neck. But we always felt safe and would shout and hulloo to him as we walked or trotted by and call him 'Silly Old Rover', 'Old Devil', 'Old Mad-dog', and 'Cranky Bill'. Yet every chain, however stout, has somewhere along its length a link weaker than its neighbour. We never thought of that, until one day, as my younger brother Wally and I were calling to him on our way to school, he suddenly broke loose!

We were just as surprised at seeing the dog break free as he was at having at long last regained freedom to run down his tormentors. We stopped still, and so did he – on his black and white canine nose. Realisation came to dog and boys simultaneously for we ran as if the fabled witch of Pluckley was after us and the dog ran too, fast and furiously, after us. How we ran, yet how our steps seemed to clog. We reached a six-barred gate into Little Marsh Field and as we fronted it I threw our small gladstone-bag high over it into the field beyond, for that bag contained our dinners. Leaping up to the top bar I jerked my younger brother up and as I fell over to the other side dragged him shouting after me, yet not soon enough, for the 'Old Devil' dog jumped and just caught his trousers, grazing his backside with its four front teeth. Indeed, a narrow escape!

*Pluckley was my playground*

*Day with its burden and heat had departed, and twilight descending*
*Brought back the evening star to the sky, and the herds to the homestead.*
*Pawing the ground they came, and resting their necks on each other,*
*And with nostrils distended inhaling the freshness of evening.*

'Evangeline', by Henry Wadsworth Longfellow

# CHAPTER THREE

At the end of the ancient right-o'-way across Honey Farm Field, was a stout stile, which gave access to Elvey Lane, which left the Pluckley-Mundy Bois-Egerton road just before the Horse and Crown was reached. This lane led then to Elvey Farm, where lived Farmer Jesse Buss, wife and the younger Buss's. From there it climbed windingly up the steep outer slopes of the Pluckley-Egerton escarpment of green sandstone until it met the Pluckley to Egerton road to the north, called the Top Road.

South along this lane were the 'Barns', composed of a huge thatched black barn, part of which served as cowsheds and pig-sheds, which the larger portion composed a stowage place for hay, straw, and threshed field pea and bean stalks. Part of this section was used as a threshing floor until as late as the 1920s where Plushey Austin and Doddie Smith, at certain times, would wield the old flails to knock out the grain from the harvested wheat straws. A real Biblical touch in a slowly growing modern countryside.

In the rickyard adjacent to the 'Barns' were open-fronted cow-byres and in one corner a round pond. It was in the thatched roof of the cow-byres where the flirting-tailed pied wagtails built their nests, year after year, seemingly quite undisturbed by our comings and goings about the place, the working visits by the farmer and his men, and the pigs and cows quartered there.

This pond held a great fascination for me, for it was in the dark-brown water of this drinking-place where I first espied one day, while returning home from school, the giant lizard. This creature, shiny black and quite nine inches long, suddenly rose to the surface, hesitated, and then swirled around and dived steeply, never to be seen again, though I often watched for an hour or more at a time for it to appear. Actually it was a triton newt, the largest of our native newts or efts, known in our district as 'effets'. These amphibious creature, common to most of the ponds in and around Pluckley, form a direct link with those gigantic saurians of prehistoric times. But what a thrill it had been to see that huge fellow come up from the water arrow-headed depths of Barn Pond!

The barn and the cow-byres were useful places in which to go bird-nesting, for besides the pied wagtails, one could find over the lintels of the open fronts of the cow-sheds and the byres such kinds as the thrush and the blackbird nesting. They would built their nests upon the lintels or upon the beams, and there, practically undisturbed except for cows, horses or pigs, and a flock of nondescript fowls, would hatch and rear their young and then, year by year, would either re-nest in the old ones, or build new ones by the side of the old. As well as these wild birds could be found the loosely-built nests of the house sparrows, thickly lined with wool and feathers, built up under the heavy thatched roof, or in works and corners, high up inside the gloomy yet always warm great barn. Now and then a robin, common wren, or a golden-crested wren would build up under the dusty straw of the thatch, and here lived huge black and shiny brown spiders, and many bats.

There is one adventure which occurred to me one evening when roaming around this building seeking for nests. Farmer Buss had a great Middle White sow corralled in a wattle-gated pen in one section of the barn. Being so used to pigs, horses, cows and sheep, I thought nothing of climbing over the wattle-gates with its pen and moving into the barn-covered portion where it slept. Suddenly this great old female pig swung about sniffing, and lumbering forward, charged me. As quick as lightning I was inside the barn and climbing upwards; hanging by fingers and toes to the stoutish lathes carrying the thatch. I dared hardly breathe and it took all of my time to refrain from sneezing from the tickling particles of ancient straw dust which had assailed my nostrils in my scrambled ascent. There I hung; minutes passed; finally the old pig went outside, baffled, yet still on the alert and listening hard.

Eventually I climbed very quietly down and warily approached the entrance. Outside the big sow stood but six feet or so away. Suddenly making up my mind, I drew a deep breath, rushed out, and swung over the nearest wattle-gate. As I cleared it and landed all asprawl beyond the pen, the bad-tempered old sow was already at the side and fiercely taking it out on the bars of the gate, tearing and champing at them with its teeth, backed by the ferocity of its ungovernable rage!

Climbing up to the roof of this barn was another of our escapades. We would climb up its steeply thatched roof to the top, then slide slowly down the other side to drop down some twenty feet, to land safely in the warm softness of an old rotted dung heap, which we called a 'maxon', below.

******

Every village around Pluckley had one or two folks who were known as 'characters' and perhaps one of Pluckley's greatest characters was Old Puddeney Weeks. At one time, before I had been born into the village, he had been a thriving butcher at Pluckley Thorne. His shop had been next to my grandparents' cottage, while his house next to his shop adjoined the inn known as the Blacksmith's Arms. Drink, of which he had partaken of far more than his share, had wrought his downfall. His business dwindled and failed and his wife, a son and daughter, left to live in the Bungalows, a row of tiny single-storied cottages, over near Mundy Bois.

Disowned by his wife and family, owing to his drunken and thriftless ways, he drifted around the village until he died at quite a ripe old age. For many years he worked for Mr Fidler, the licensee of the Black Horse at Pluckley village. He helped with the horses and in the stables, for Mr Fidler ran the horse-coach to and from Pluckley Station, and did carrying and haulage work, as well as supplying horses and hearse for village funerals. Old Puddeney was as tough as old leather, and on one occasion he stuck a prong of a pitchfork clean through the palm of one of his hands, the point protruding from the back. He immediately got some warm horse dung from one of the horse-stables, slapped it on the back and palm of the injured hand, then tied it up tightly in an old red kerchief. This he left on for several days, and when finally he removed it and the now hardened dung, the wound had healed up beautifully. Gaffer Turff said at the time that if it had been anyone else but Old Weeks, then death from tetanus would probably have resulted from such strange doctoring! Old Weeks drank like a fish and chewed tobacco as consistently as a cow chews the cud. He never spat out the tobacco-impregnated spittle he made, but swallowed it! When he grew tired of chewing his 'quid' of baccy he spat it into his ramshackle old soft trilby hat and stuck it back on his bald pate until needed.

Perhaps the most peculiar adventure that ever happened to the solid old drunkard was when, coming back from the Rose and Crown one snowy winter's night, he pitched headlong into the Barn Pond and crashed through the quite thick ice into the icy water. For two whole days he was missing. He had been, for some time past, living and sleeping in the old barn. When he did not show up for work, for he was doing odd job work for Farmer Buss at this particular period, the farmer went down to see where he had got to. Old Weeks' 'spoor marks' of the previous night had been almost obliterated with snow. In the iced surface of the pond gaped a large jagged hole. Immediately help was brought in; the ice was broken all around and dragging operations with long-handled hay rakes began: but no body could be found! Then the searchers suddenly discovered that, hanging upon the great double-door of the barn, were certain garments. Old Weeks' battered hat, his great-coat, coat, waistcoat and trousers, as well as his woollen vest and long pants. His boots were on the ground. But where was the old chap? Evidently he had tripped over the raised brickwork encircling two sides of the pond and, cracking through the ice, had come up in the hole he had made, scrambled ashore, taken off his sodden clothes, hung them upon the door, and then disappeared quite naked! He was nowhere in the barn, sheds or byres. He had not returned to his family's home at the Bungalows; he had not contacted Mr Cooper, the landlord of the Rose and Crown; nor had he been to the nearest habitation, old Mr Austin's place at Honey Farm. For two days a fruitless search went on. Opinion said: 'When we do find him, he'll be dead, and stiffer than a frozen cow turd!' Yet, lo and behold, upon the morning of the third day he came to light, emerging warm and dry and quite fit and well from the interior of a nearby straw-stack where he had been all the time. He had pulled out sufficient straw to make a cosy nest inside and had then pulled in as much of the displaced straw as he could manage after him, and had slept the sleep of the just and of dormice, for two whole days!

******

At the back of the Elvey Lane Barn was a field called Barn Field, and in it, in one secluded corner near to the barn, was a piece of rush- and reed-edged water known as Barnfield Pond. Here one could watch, on quiet warm afternoons in summer, the sleek-coated water rats swimming about and busily eating the tender shoots and roots of aquatic plants. Here too, a pair of moorhens nested in the large clump of bulrushes, and this well-hidden, dampish nest supplied us with many eggs which we would boil in a clean tin can over a camp fire in a very small spinney, called Little Shave, near our house at Mundy Bois. Close to this pond stood an oak tree supposedly haunted by a ghost which could fly! So one night I went to see if such was the case, only to find that the flying ghost was a barn owl that had its home in a hollow part of the tree about twelve feet above the ground. My going there disturbed it and it flew out upon its noiseless pinions, swooped and flew ghostlike into the gathering mists of oncoming night. The following year I found the nest of this owl and put my head into the hollow before the bird had left, getting a very severe parrot-like peck for my pains. The beak of a barn owl is a sharp and formidable weapon and its claws are worse! One lived and learned in those days.

******

Yet the giant lizard and the spiteful and bad-tempered sow were all outweighed by a very vicious white leghorn cock who lorded it over the motley seraglio of nondescript hens of whom we called him the Sultan. Time and time again he attacked people from his hiding place in the hedge, and at length the children who, in summer, would make this their short route home from school at Pluckley, forsook this shorter cut to go home by a longer way round. This cocky old cock I thought must be taught a lesson, so equipping myself with a very long wild bramble from a hedge I went down the lane to meet his lordship. Sure enough, out he came and made a dash at my legs, attempting to peck my calves and failing. He suddenly jumped up, throwing out his legs, and tried to bring them downwards upon my legs so as to nip them with his long spurs. I ran, and he followed, and then I swung the long spiky bramble at his neck. The brambles caught in his neck feathers, fluffed out in anger, and I had him tethered fast! I pulled backwards, and so tightened the spines more severely, and then he had to follow me, like an unwilling dog hanging upon a lead. I walked him from the old Elvey Barn right to the top of Elvey Lane near to the inn, then let him go. He was too tired and mortified to scurry back, but went down the lane slowly and humiliated. Never again did he attack anyone, and the youngsters, including myself, could again walk free from fear of that pestilential fowl! He would watch us from the hedge, but never set upon us. He would lower his head in shame at the memory of his humiliation and the villain he had once been.

*Scatter as from an unextinguished hearth*
*Ashes and sparks, my words among mankind!*
*Be through my lips to unawakened earth*
*The trumpet of a prophecy! O, wind,*
*If winter comes, can spring be far behind?*

'Ode to the West Wind' by Percy Bysshe Shelley

# CHAPTER FOUR

The Pinnock Field along Elvey Lane, in one of its sides adjoined, in one part, the old barn and yard mentioned in the former chapter. In this field it was, when I found my first chaffinch's nest, and also my first nests of the long-tailed tit and that glorious small songster the black-cap warbler. Back in the 1850s and for many years afterwards the stream and pond must have yielded much of the water needed by the cattle of those far-off days. Where the old stream had curled its way hundreds of years ago, some now forgotten farmer had had it widened and deepened. A brickwork and ragstone bridge had been built over the stream near the lane, under which it flowed, the lane being carried over the stream by a road-bridge. In this particular corner near the collection of cow-byres and the huge barn, two ponds collected water which, when full, emptied their surplus into the nearby stream. These ponds must have been dug out and enlarged from water-filled depressions well over a hundred years before. When the stream swung round near to one corner of the stack yard, large fragments of Bethersden marble could be seen where a pathway or pavement had been made, no doubt for the farm hands to stand upon when drawing water from the stream. These paving stones, quarried and worked at the old stone or 'marble' quarries of Bethersden in years gone by, are very durable and almost impervious to the weather. From this marble was furnished paving stones for side walks in nearby villages, and for fonts in churches, one of which can be seen in the church at Harrietsham village about ten miles from Pluckley. Another use for this fossiliferous stone, composed almost entirely of fossil freshwater molluscs, was the manufacture of gravestones, many of which can still be seen, almost untouched by the weather of nearly two centuries, in such churchyards as those of Pluckley, Little Chart, Bethersden, Charing, Egerton and Ulcombe. There were, at one time, several quarries in the Bethersden area; one at Great Chart and another at Boughton Malherbe.

It was in this large field, seldom traversed by folks around, where wild rabbits made the shorter type of burrows in the open meadow. More than one plump rabbit have I caught from these short excavations; by thrusting one's arm down these holes the length was determined. If it was a very short burrow, and the rabbit was at home, you felt its fur. Then you grabbed it by its ears, drew it forth and killed it by striking it hard with the outer edge of the hand where the backbone ends near the base of the skull. This particular spot, according to our headmaster Gaffer Turff, was called the *medulla oblongata*, and was the meeting-place of all the vital nerves. This portion of the rabbit's anatomy was known to us boys as Old Medulla's Oblong Garter! When the burrow was deeper, a long and stout branch of the wild blackberry was used. This was first poked into the hole until its progress was halted, either by the end of the burrow or by the rabbit if in residence. You could always tell by the feel of the resistance to the briar if a rabbit was in the hole, then one would turn the spiny branch round and round to catch it in the fur of the rabbit, to pull it out and then administer the *coup de grace*.

******

North of Pinnock Field is Three Oaks Meadow, named after the three great trees of that name that grew there, in a row, across the central part of the field. But they have been cut down there many years and only their weathering bases can now be seen. They were very high, and their branches grew far out, and had given shelter to scores of generations of cows, horses and sheep. Only one of them was it possible to climb, as the lower branches grew too far up the great boles of the other two. Even the climbable one was only so to me. On one side were half a dozen protuberances to which I was able to not so much hold as to hang on to – like a leech – with my fingertips. At the very top of this giant oak we had, for several years, observed the large nest of a pair of magpies. No-one had never 'taken' that nest, for no-one could climb to it. How well I remember that particular Sunday back in 1923, when I made up my mind to reach that nest so high above my head.

The early spring leafage had not entirely shrouded the magpie's nest from view, and I began the ascent about 12.30 on my way home from church. It took me over half an hour to reach the nest held in position by the very topmost branches of the oak. The birds were not at home, and all I found within the great ball of twigs were some broken egg-shells of the previous year. I discovered that the magpie was quite a builder, for the nest had a canopy or roof of twigs over the bowl of the nest and shaped so as to drain off most of the moisture caused by rain. We had seen the pair of magpies in the preceding year at their home, but this year of 1923 we saw them not, nor did they ever reside there again. Getting back to earth was even harder than the ascent and far more dangerous, and it was 1.30 in the afternoon before I dropped the last few feet to the meadow below. I was blackened, pricked and scratched and utterly tired out, but it had been a very worthwhile adventure, because it had been hard and tough as well as dangerous.

Here, in Three Oaks Meadow, in the springtime, nested some two dozen pairs of lapwings, or as we called them, plovers, or pee-wits. When we went in search of their nests they would fly to other parts of the field and swoop and cry over spots where their nests were not, to distract us from where the nests were really situated. Sometimes they would swoop down on us, crying loudly, and pretend to attack our heads, but at the last moment would wheel aside and fly up into the sky to begin the course of a new and noisier attack. On one occasion one of these crafty birds even pretended it had a crippled wing and fluttered along the ground trying to get us to chase it. But we were wise to the tricks of these lapwings and heeded it not. Perhaps the best way of all of finding their nests was to come across an adjoining field and lie quietly behind the intervening hedgerow. Through this we could watch these birds, check their settling-down points and then mark them by picking upon something near to them, such as a tall tuft of grass, a bunch of rushes, a tall thistle or maybe an old branch. Then we would go round the other side of the hedge into Three Oaks Meadow and taking straight lines to the particular objects, memorised beforehand, could usually walk directly to the nest. The eggs of these lapwings are quite large and very rich eating. Our usual procedure was to boil them or fry them, in our old Scouts' billy-can over a hissing fire of dry sticks, and eat them under the shelter of sheep pens, made natural by nature, and modified at sheep-shearing time by the shearers.

It was in the field next to Three Oaks Meadow where this pen was situated. Two old trails or rights-o'-way converged at one point here: the Mundy Bois-to-Pluckley Thorne and the Mundy Bois-to-Pluckley village trails. The field in which the sheep pen was we called Plateau Field, not because it was any higher than the fields about it, but because a plateau is usually a very flat spot. This field was rich in white clover, and in the early 1920s white clover seed, after being threshed, fetched very high prices. In fact 1920 and 1921 found other small golden seeds making a price of £1 per pound of seed. A crushed bone fertiliser could be hand-spread over this field in the early spring, especially if the weather was inclined to be wet, and make the whole locality stink to high heaven! Certainly a contrast to the delicate perfume of the clover blooms later on in the year.

Where the two trails met was a five-barred gate giving access to Plateau Field which had to be crossed before reaching the old Mundy Bois road, where the Mundy Bois cottages stood all in a row. The five-barred gate formed one end of the sheep-pen, the open end gave way to the field. On either side high hedges, with a few trees, drew wild, and the upper branches had grown over, interlocked and formed a solid natural roof over the area of the pen. Inside, especially on a dullish day, a peculiar twilight held sway, and in rainy weather one could stay in this old sheep-pen without getting wet at all! At sheep-shearing and lambs' tail cutting time, the farmhands would erect wattle-gates across the open end to full enclose this naturally made sheepfold. Here the sometimes protesting sheep would be shorn of their fleeces, and the shearers would become lousey with sheep ticks, which horrible flat-bodied insects would leave the sheep and burrow under the skins of the shearers. These ticks had to be cut out when the labourers got home before they had their baths, disinfected with Condy's Fluid! Here in this pen the bleating lambs would have their tails docked by having them placed upon a block of hard wood to be severed by a razor-sharp knife. Nearby a pot of boiling pitch was kept on the simmer and the bleeding stumps of the lambs' tails were painted and cauterised with the hot black fluid and that was how the lambs lost their tails – primitive, but quite decent really, and it was most sure, effective and hygienic in its simple way.

\*\*\*\*\*\*

On the further side of Plateau Field is the long strip of narrow woodland called the Shave, sometimes referred to the as the Mundy Bois Road Wood. Beyond this wood is the Mundy Bois Road leading to

Greenhill and the Top Road which links Egerton with Pevington and Pluckley. This wood is composed of oak trees with tough grasses and dwarf maythorn bushes for underwood. It was here in this shave where I saw my first peregrine falcon, having disturbed it as it rested in one of the oak trees. This beautiful hawk had never been seen in this locality before, and when it took off it flew fast away in the direction of Ashford, no doubt having strayed so far inland from the cliffs of Folkestone where these hawks have been seen and found nesting. On a low bank that ran along the field side of this narrow wood of which it formed part, grew a springy little oak sapling that afforded me great pleasure in gale weather. For I would climb up as far as I could go with safety, and then, holding hard to the topmost part, would let the fierce bursts of wind sway the oak sapling to and fro under my weight. Thus I would stay, thrilling to the far-swinging side-to-side action of the tree, my face whipped with the rushing air and my senses enthralled by the thought that perhaps the next great gust would throw my weight too far and the top would splinter and give way, throwing me down to earth! Many were the happy hours I spent climbing high-up into those straight growing oaks, after the numerous nests of the tree sparrows and of the house sparrows also. These latter birds would nest in these oaks when housing and barn accommodation was overcrowded by their kind in the near vicinity. There were so many nests, all containing so many eggs, and almost every egg dissimilar with variations of brown or black splotches, specks, and markings. At one end of the Shave a wasps' nest came to light almost every year in the bank of the deep ditch, overgrown with long dry grasses. Then, when the nest of these black-and-yellow robbers had been located we would wait for a dark night, when Arthur Collins and his brother Jack, two hefty young men who lived in No. 5 Mundy Bois Cottages, opposite the Shave, would swiftly dig out as much of the bank around the tiny entrance of the wasps' nest as they could before the angry inhabitants could fully realise what was afoot. As soon as the first few score of sleepy wasps had emerged the brothers would throw in a large quantity of liquid pitch and then set it afire. The suffocating smoke and fumes would be conducted down the tunnel into the large nesting chamber in the bank where reposed the nest of paper-like wood-pulp made by the wasps. This nest, as large as a football, full of wasps and their grubs, all potential wasps, would soon be rendered useless, full of fumes and the dead bodies of countless numbers of these orchard-fruit thieves, and murderers of honey-bees who they killed for their bags of pollen. The next day the nest would be dug out and any survivors put to a quick death.

In this wood I made my early efforts at pioneering, by cutting down the very small saplings with a jagged edge old bill-hook or wood-chopper and making a bivouac. A fire of old sticks from the trees would be lit and the ashes allowed to accumulate. Then the glowing embers would be raked away to form a circle to show a patch of hot burnt earth. Upon the scorching soil the eggs of moorhens would be placed, and sometimes a few eggs of the partridge if luck had favoured me. Then the circle of warm ashes would be drawn over the eggs. Half an hour later these ashes would be raked away and the eggs underneath would be ready for eating, just as if they had been hard-boiled! And how good they tasted, washed down with a beer-bottle of water taken from the old spring in the ditch, just down the road, nearly opposite to Brown's Kitchen House, that had been a lovely farm in this region a hundred years ago!

*It is one of the blessings of
wilderness life that it shows us
how few things we need in order
to be perfectly happy.*

Horace Kephart

# CHAPTER FIVE

The narrow strip of woodland which extended from Little Mundy Bois Farm to just beyond the Mundy Bois Cottages was the scene of many 'battles' during my early days in this lovely hamlet. At that time, the years 1920 and 1921 saw some very spirited encounters in this wood of tall oaks. Little Mundy Bois Farm was then farmed by one of the district's old-time farmers, a Mr Turk, who was of a very miserly disposition. I remember my grandfather speaking of him and making me laugh at the idea of his extreme scrimping and saving. He had once explained to grandad how he saved his money. To him he had said: 'Lookee yurr, Jesse! I have bread an' cheese for breakfast; bread an' cheese for dinner; bread an' cheese for tea, but I down't have no supper for parson says "light suppers make long life" and I reckon if I don't have any suppers I'll live a-sight longer and save money too!'

This woodland warfare usually took place when my chums Bob and John Beale came down from Prebbles Hill Farm to play at my place. Most times it would be Bob and myself holding the wood against the 'enemy' in the shape of his brother 'Long John', 'Blunt' Sharp and my younger brother Walter. The enemy would go away to gather clods of earth; when enough ammunition had been found Bob and I would retire into the Shave and the enemy force would come down the road and try to locate us. Then they would bombard us and try to get into the Shave and evict us. That never happened, for not only had we the protection of the trees but also the screen of the high thick bramble-covered hedge on our side, as well as the deep wide ditch, knee-deep in rotting leaves which ran under it. When some movement in the road betrayed their position, how heartily would the 'Germans' pound us with their clod-earth 'shells'. The lumps of hard earth of Weald clay would crash around us, flattening themselves against the tree-trunks to shower us with 'shrapnel'. We would retaliate against the 'Allemands' and they, in the open, strung out along the road, had to jump and run to avoid the unseen artillery hammering at them from the wood. It was all good rough fun, though now and then the attackers and the defenders caught unlucky smacks which showered them with earth and dust, and left a bump, bruise or a few scratches upon their bodies.

\*\*\*\*\*\*

The five cottages at Mundy Bois formed a row very near the edge of the road. We called them the Mundy Bois Cottages, yet my Uncle Harry over at Pluckley said their real name was Pinchcrust Cottages, which I truly believe they had been named. For Pinchcrust is like other peculiar countryside names of this type, such as Starve-gut Farm, and over at Newlands Lane, Little Chart, when Jeanne de Casalis the famous stage actress came to live in after years, the old house she took over, improved and modernised was called Hunger Hatch in the old days. My grandmother, who had lived as a milkmaid in her youth at Ragged House Farm, across the fields from our cottages, told me that these cottages had been called, at a time when gipsies and an old dealer had lived in them, as Tickle-Belly Alley! This too, was true, for some of the gipsy maidens had been the mistresses of certain local men in the surrounding parishes in those now far-off days. Though called cottages, these habitations were high and very well-proportioned, putting to shame some of the places in the district known as houses. It is surprising how, over the years, families come and go, even in remote and scanty parish communities. So it will be well to record here, who lived in these cottages, when, in December 1919 our family moved from Pluckley into the middle or No. 3 cottage.

At No.1 lived old Mr Austin and his daughter Polly or Por, and her little daughter. In No.2 resided, amidst her aspidistras, geraniums and six cats, old Mercy Fowle (Merce) who had come down in the world many years before. Her father had been one of the most prosperous farmers at Egerton, owning Ragged House Farm, and he had also had built, just up the road from our cottages, a very large and beautiful residence known as Appleby Grange. The Fowles had gone bankrupt and Mercy had been forced to live in the cottage. She kept a few score fowls, living mostly on their eggs, and selling those she did not use to people round about. She lived a hard, hermit-like life and we often wondered how she kept body and soul together. But she was tough woman, all bones, skin and whipcord muscles. My grandmother, after she had married her Jesse and gone to live at one of the two pretty little red-brick cottages at Mundy Bois crossroads, told us how, after the young Fowle girls had left Ragged House Farm to live at the wonderful new house, they would put on 'such airs and graces' and never deign to notice the former Miss Heild (my grandma) who had worked so hard and such long hours at Ragged House Farm as their father's milk-maid for one shilling and sixpence and her keep. 'How are the mighty fallen!' Gran would exclaim, quoting Holy Writ.

In No.4 lived Mrs Hart, widowed daughter of old Farmer Batt of Britcher Farm up on the slopes of Greenhill (in Egerton parish) to the north of us. She did from tuberculosis in 1923 leaving three little boys. She was buried at Bethersden, about five miles from Mundy Bois as this parish was the true home of the Batt family. It was a cold day, with a blustery wind and torrential rain. That morning I had cycled over to Charing, a small country 'town' five miles to the north, to bring back a wreath of tulips subscribed for by her friends and neighbours. In the end cottage, No.5, dwelt Mr and Mrs George Collins and their two tall sons and their daughter Violet (Vi) who was only thirteen but a fine strapping girl who would have passed muster as a woman of twenty years. It was Mrs Collins who nursed Mrs Hart in her illness and who had been with her to the very last. On the morning following Mrs Hart's death, Mrs Collins asked me if I would like to see her. I went in, and there she lay, still and peaceful, her pale finely cut face with its transparent skin calm and beautiful, for she had been a lovely-looking woman of fairy-like beauty in the days before her long, last illness. 'Touch her forehead with your finger' said her old friend. I did so. The coolness came through the skin at my finger ends. 'Isn't she peaceful?' asked Mrs Collins. 'The dead can't harm you, sonny,' she said, as she shewed me to the cottage door.

******

Just past the cottages, bordering the edge of the road was situated a strip of light woodland in which a few oaks grew amidst high blackthorn and maythorn trees. The rest of this tiny wood was a tangle of wild briars. We called it the 'Little Shave' and it became, in the course of time, one of our near-to-home camping places. From the road this wood presented an impenetrable aspect, until one day, in 1920, I saw a member of a local family, with a shot-gun under his arm, just disappear through the high thorny frontage festooned with clutching briars. The next day I visited this spot and found that a way had been cut through just there and the outer branches allowed to grow wild to conceal the entrance to a small pathway. Going in I discovered that this path traverses the wood from end to end, finishing where a grew mount of wild brambles grew. Evidently it was here, in this tiny shave or small wood, where the father and his boys stood in waiting at its western boundary for rabbits to appear in the adjoining field which they shot for their cooking pot! Such types of poaching were prevalent in all the parishes around. A shot would be heard, yet no-one seen. The marksmen would note where the rabbit had been killed, and after dark would retrieve it.

This Little Shave soon belonged to us lads, though the above-mentioned family did not care to share it with us. In the very centre of it we set up camp where four small trees grew. We roofed it over with sticks and roughly thatched it with hay and ivy. We made a fireplace of stones and set it just beyond where we could sit in shelter on old buckets we had found in a rubbish heap in the southern end of the shave. Here we would boil our tea or cocoa, and cook wild birds' eggs, and neatly-plucked fat sparrows on a long spit which we covered with dripping when roasted and shook on pepper and salt and ate them, washing them down with scalding tea without milk or sugar in it. Then came a day when, after a squabble, my brother Walter and his friend Jack Luckhurst whose father had bought Little Mundy Bois Farm from old Mr Turk, took it into their heads to break away from myself and the Beales and our camp and set up one in the Little Shave for themselves.

This could not be tolerated, so one quiet afternoon I set fire to their rival camp and burned it to the ground. Then I set fire to the camp I had made and stood beneath the blazing rood between the trees, to feel how that unknown Roman soldier had perhaps felt in Pompeii so many hundreds of years ago when he had stood still on guard while the red-hot ashes from Vesuvius in eruption had fallen around him and the sea of slowly-moving lava had borne down to his guard post, where he died. Then, in our more modern times his remains were discovered as Pompeii became uncovered through the efforts of famous archaeologists, and his memory enshrined in a painting by a famous artist, and called 'Faithful Unto Death'. I ended up with my cap burned full of holes and tiny burn blisters on the backs of my hands. After this incendiarism the old camp was rebuilt, and the rival camp rose not again. The rival campers came back and once more peace reigned in our domain. This camp became very popular with all of us, and even in the dark evenings of winter we would, after tea, resort to it, building a fine fire and putting on the tea can. We had an old bicycle lamp of the oil burning type and this, with the glow from the fire, enabled us to sit there and read our papers and comics, chief amongst them the *Magnet* (of Billy Bunter fame), *The Boys' Friend*, *Boys Magazine*, *Chips*, *Comic Cuts* and *Funny Wonder*.

In the centre of this wood, hard by the camp, grew a thin tall tree that we used as a route-cut point. Wherever possible we fortified all the immediate area and around this permanent camp with blackthorn branches placed in a circle, something like the 'boma' thrown up by explorers and hunters for their night camps in wildest Africa to keep out prowling lions.

Extending from the eastern edge of this shave grew a huge mound of brambles that became an adventurous playing spot for us. During the school holidays in the summer of 1920 I had spent two weeks with old Mercy Fowle hop-picking at Mr Wood's place, Park Farm, on the other side of Smarden Forest on the Frith (shown on the Ordnance Survey as Dering Wood), where I earned nineteen shillings and sixpence.

Ten shillings of this I gave to my mother, and on the rest I took the train to Ashford and purchased the *Greyfriars Holiday Annual* at six shillings, went to the cinema and had tea in the town, with enough left over to purchase a small pot of honey for mother as a little present. In this annual there was an articled called 'How a picture play is made', by a well-known producer. This came in useful. I made a tripod of sticks with a flat top to which I secured a large cardboard box, with a cocoa tin set in the front as the lens. There was no cranking-handle, the 'cameraman' just went through the motions. Our first film was called *The Runaway Express*. The action consisted of one of us getting into an old pram and being propelled down a short slope into the great bramble mound. The 'express train' would hit the bramble patch and then shoot the occupant into the air to land safely but in a rather prickly position on top of the brambles. Everyone would have a turn at being in the runaway express and also as cameraman. After this we made a 'film' called *The Battle of Wipers* (Ypres) which consisted of some of us lying in a ditch and being bombarded with grassy clods by the enemy. What finally ended our cinematic adventures was when three of us were in the old pram going full belt down the gentle slope of the road from the cottages to the sharp head not far from Brown's Kitchen House. The cameraman was to 'shoot' the scene from the middle of the road and just before the speeding pram got to the camera a quick jerk was to be made by the driver which would alter the course of the pram to the left of the cameraman and so leave him and the camera intact. But as the pram bore down upon the camera even the efforts of all the occupants could not make it turn. The pram hit the camera and its operator for a terrific 'six', overturned, and the riders hit the road in every conceivable position. After that, though we retained our old pram for other adventures, we quitted the world of the silver screen and decided that film acting would be rather painful.

*When ice all melted in the sun,*
*And left the wavy streams to run,*
*We longed, as summer came, to roll*
*In river foam, o'er depth and shoal;*
*And if we lost our loose-bowed swing*
*We had a kite to pull our string:*
      *Or, if no ball*
      *Would rise or fall*
*With us, another joy was nigh*
*Before our joy all passed us by.*

'Joy Passing By' by William Barnes

# CHAPTER SIX

During the times, particularly those of earlier date, when I was at school and even afterwards up to early 1926, camping-places of a permanent character were made and forks (strong points of strategic use) and lookouts were made and kept up by myself and the Beales. They afforded us resting-places and hideaways. In them we held councils of war; used them for cooking food and storing odds and ends useful to our ramblings and our 'raids'. Gradually these spots grew in a line to form a complete 'Roman Wall' from Smarden Forest south of Mundy Bois and separating lands and farms on the Egerton side from those of Pevington and Pluckley on the other. Working from the forest in the south to Pluckley village to the north, in sequence, I will outline these forks and camps and so as the reader may have some idea as to how they grew and became linked up, the approximate times and the years will be appended to them.

In the southern part of the Smarden Forest we had a spot called Fir Trees Hide. To the north of this great woodland on the banks of a deep stream was Forest Fort, where we spent much of our time in the good weather and where we learned to handle our bows and arrows. The next place was half a mile away, in the Shave at Mundy Bois, known as Pioneer Camp. Then at the bottom of our garden we had a summer camp called Grey Wolf Camp. This was an 'under-canvas' camp as we had a small portable bivouac tent as our headquarters. Not far away, in the adjoining field to the cottages, was a mound on which grew an ash tree in which an owl at evening would often sit. This was known as Lone Owl Lookout. From here we could scan the surrounding fields to good advantage. The next meeting-place was what came to be called Fire Camp in the Little Shave. Then down the Mundy Bois to Greenhill road we had a camp in an old brick-built hoppers' kitchen of the early Victorian era. This we named Brown's Kitchen Camp.

About quarter of a mile to the north of this was a large pond hidden in a deep depression on the lower gentle slopes of Greenhill. Here in the summer we met to paddle and swim, sail boats and rest and laze around. When the pond was frozen over in winter we had one long slide there and often skated after darkness had descended. This spot was called Lost Pond Camp. Then going north-east about a quarter of a mile we had Explorer's Camp in the eastern end of Mundy Bois Wood, near to Pevington. This was a woodman's hut I had discovered during the summer of 1920, and which we kept in repair right up till I left the district. It was made of wood-poles and thatched with hay and brushwood. Inside we had sawn blocks of woods for seats. But a stone's throw from this was an open-camp for fine weather and the nearby pond, used by Farmer Strang's ducks, was a handy bathing place. The ducks would often travel across the fields from Greenhill Farm to spend a day in and around this pond, and usually they would lay a few eggs for us which we fed right royally upon! This spot we named Duck Camp.

Working still further round into the east we had another lookout in a small depression high on the Elvey Lane slopes called Pebble Lookout. Then we took over the Greensand escarpment from where the fair Weald of Kent could be reviewed in all its quiet beauty. Here on this rocky escarpment and below in its almost impenetrable jungle at the base we had the following meeting-places in line as far as Prebbles Hill about a mile from Pluckley village itself. Steepcliff Camp; Brownwater Lookout, called sometimes Tree-stump Lookout; Badgers' Hide, consisting of an old badger's lair from which the badgers had been evicted by Farmer Buss and his men in 1921, after much laborious digging. Thus they had left and the blackthorn bushes had covered in the top entrance. Into this place Bob Beale and myself would crawl and working downwards underground would emerge upon a tiny track upon the almost sheer face of this escarpment.

Then came a break in this line of cliff where a great landslide well beyond living memory had once taken place. Then the cliff-like formation carried on and round to quite near Prebbles Hill Farm, the home of the Beales. At its eastern extremity we had a fine fortified camp halfway up the cliff on a broad section of rock. This was known, owing to its impregnability, as The Fort. Not far from here was Rock Hide, on the slopes overlooking the lower long meadow of Mr Beale's farm. Very close to Pluckley village we had a meeting-place named Hidden Camp, right in the very centre of a dense fir tree plantation, one of the game preserves belonging to Sir Henry Dering, baronet of Surrenden Mansion and the squire and virtual overlord of Pluckley parish.

How his fine old port-tinted nose would have been inflamed if he had known! Nearby, in a very tall wind-twisted pine tree we had a fine lookout known, of course, as Pine Tree Lookout. A few hundred yards away, near Westfield Steps, and overlooking the village street along all its length, were some large laurel trees into which we would climb and watch unseen the comings and the goings of the villagers, like silent Red Indians watching some fort or small township, in the old Wild West of years ago. This was Laurel Lookout.

The times of the making of the foregoing camps, forts and lookouts are as follows:

Fir Trees Hide (1923), Forest Fort (1922), Pioneer Camp (1921), Grey Wolf Camp (1921), Lone Owl Lookout (1920), Fire Camp

(1920), Brown's Kitchen Camp (1920), Lost Pond Camp (1920), Explorer's Camp (1920), Duck Camp (1920), Pebble Lookout (1923), Steepcliff Camp (1921), Brownwater or Tree-stump Lookout (1922), Badgers' Hide (1922), The Fort (1920), Rock Hide (1923), Hidden Camp (1920), Pine Tree Lookout (1921), Laurel Lookout (1920).

We were so often in trouble with the farmers such as Farmer Strang of Greenhill Farm, or Farmer Batt of Britcher Farm (Egerton), our sworn 'enemy'. Then there was Farmer Buss of Elvey Farm who, like Farmer Strang, was one of our friendliest 'enemies' and Captain Len Slaughter of Mundy Bois Farm who also drops into the same category. Our feuds were long, our skirmishes many, but I think they really enjoyed the fun of chasing us all over the countryside!

*Pluckley was my playground*

*Whenever you see a wild animal in the wood go towards him carelessly. Let the creature know that you have seen him, and then suddenly change your course or do something to show you are not apparently interested in him.*
*He knows that you saw him and yet went about your own business without offering to harm him.*
*That animal will never forget you.*

*Alone in the Wilderness* by Joseph Knowles

# CHAPTER SEVEN

One of our greatest playing places during the years 1920 to 1923 was the deep, circular piece of water we called Garden Pond that was situated at the end of the three long gardens of the first three cottages of the Mundy Bois Cottages. Part of its western shoreline ran out into Batt's Meadow to form a shallow extension when the pond was really full, which became, as the summer advanced, a miniature flat of black mud criss-crossed by sun-cracked fissures. Nearly all the fields and meadows around abounded, in the warmer seasons, with grass snakes and slow-worms, called 'slay-worms' in the local dialect. These small animals of the reptilian order were neither snakes nor worms, but legless lizards and quite harmless, just as were the very often three feet-long grass snakes. It was a rare sight to see these snakes swimming about the pond with their sinuous side-to-side motion of propulsion. They came to this quiet water to search for and hunt the frogs and newts, and if by luck perhaps a baby moorhen or two. These creatures they would catch, and the newts they would swallow tail-first and any hapless frogs or tiny moorhens.

Each year a pair of moorhens nested somewhere deep under the masses of woody nightshade and belladonna that grew all over the borderline of the south-west corner. It was a wonderful thrill to lie and wait for the parent birds to bring out sometimes as many as nine or ten fluffy black chicks who swam in line astern of the old birds back and forth across the pond. This old pond had for many generations supplied ample water for the cottagers for their gardens, and of generations long passed away even beyond the oldest living memory of these days for drink for sheep and cows, and at hop-picking times in the long ago water for washing and drinking for the pickers who might be encamped about for hop-picking that lasted a month to six weeks, so great was the acreage of those hop-fields of yore.

In this patch of water thousands of newts lived and thrived, though no fish were ever seen in its yellow-muddy waters. There had been a time when I had caught stickle-backs in the clear waters of Barn Pond close by the farmyard of Mr Small who had Pinnock Farm over at Pluckley a mile away across the fields, and also roach from the lovely Chapel-field Pond a few hundred yards further over from Pinnock Farm. These fish I had transported in jugs some mile and a quarter from Pluckley Pinnock crossroads to Garden Pond, where I had loosed them, yet nothing ever came of my efforts to get fish to live in it. No doubt the moorhens, the grass snakes and certain carnivorous underwater insect life captured and ate them.

What fun we had in the early summer, when the pond was still really full, and we would kneel upon the grassy bank, some two feet above the water's level, and beat the surface vigorously with hedge stakes until the cool water flew up into our faces, drenching our hair, and soaking out shirts with its fountain-line freshness, like the hands of angels, patting and soothing our warm young bodies.

It was in the summer of 1923 when the Cuthberts, who had a bungalow and smallholding on the old road between our cottages and Appleby Grange, had a visitor for three weeks in the person of a youth about my own age. He was a nephew of 'Old Pete' as we called Mr Peter Cuthbert, and came from Reading where his parents had a grocery business. We became fast friends and wandered all over the surrounding countryside. I showed him our secret camps and hides and all the other interesting things dear to country lads, though he was, to all interests, a 'townie' as we named lads who lived in towns. A 'townie' to us free country boys was a slightly lower form of animal life than a 'villager', who resided in a village, a 'built-up area' to us in those days. His name was Jack Payne, and we swapped and read each other's comics and papers, among them being those fine old coloured comics *The Rainbow*, *Tiger Tim's Weekly* and *Bubbles*. Then there were others like *The Jester*, *The Butterfly*, *The Golden Penny* and *The Monster Comic*. Then we had our weekly boys' papers such as the pink-covered *Boys' Magazine* and *The Wizard*, *Adventure*, *Rover*, *Pluck*, *The Popular* and *Nelson Lee*.

Jack became so fascinated with the ponds around us, of which there were at least two dozen contained in an area roughly a mile by a mile, that he sent instructions home for a clockwork Atlantic liner he had never had the chance to use. It arrived a few days later, and if it had never been used previously it was given plenty of usage as soon as it arrived at The Bungalow. It did not retain its mercantile status for long, for it soon became a troopship with lead soldiers in scarlet uniforms tied with cotton to its funnels, masts and superstructures. This liner was a foot and a half from stem to stern and when fully wound could easily cross the pond under its full load of Victorian infantry, all red and dark with spiked helmets.

We sailed the troopship from a mythical place in Africa, called Mombanga, to the war front, in the east side of the pond, named Zulu Mountain. As the troopship ploughed its way across to the battle zone, Jack and myself, as a battery of enemy artillery, would open fire on it from the south shore and try, with the aid of small pieces of hard clay broken from the bank, to head it off so that it drifted aground on the Black Death Mud Flats opposite. Gradually the troopship, after several days, became shorn of masts, funnels, and some of the superstructure. It was dented and scratched, yet fully seaworthy, though the poundings it had taken had distorted its lines and this had caused trouble in the engine-room. Some of the infantry had been lost overboard, posted as 'missing, believed killed'. Others more fortunate had only lost legs, arms, rifles or heads.

Then one afternoon, with the sun blazing down, the troopship *Red Warrior* made its last voyage. With its war-scarred cargo of soldiers, some with heads fixed on with matchsticks, it slowly jerked its way out of Mombanga, heading out to sea. As soon as it had cleared the harbour it was assailed with a terrific fusillade of shells. It rocked and shuddered under the fierce assault, and its engines gave out and it lay motionless upon the shining waters in the centre of the pond. We decided that the war had gone on long enough. The *Red Warrior* must not reach Zulu Mountain with its relief column. We tore off large pieces of the sun-baked clay from the bank and soon the water boiled with huge 'shells' bursting around the troopship. When we found our aim the hard clay lumps burst all over the ship, scattering the superstructure and the soldiers all over the place amidst clouds of flying clay earth and dust. We ceased fire to take stock of her as she lay drifting so very slowly sideways, with nearly all the paintwork gone, and twisted and dented very badly. The red-coated soldiers of the Queen lay scattered over her soiled decks. Many others had been blown overboard by the 'explosions'.

We saw that the starboard decking amidships had sprung away from the side, leaving a gaping wound: a vulnerable point. Again the warm dry air resounded to our cries of 'Ready! FIRE!' and the heavy shelling began once more. The missiles pushed in the side further and further. The deck began to buckle. As the heavy clay 'shells' hit her weak spot time after time, the gallant ship rocked from port over to starboard and back again, continuously. The starboard side was repeatedly pushed under the water, which gushed into the vessel. When we saw the water had now taken command we ceased our efforts and then, bit by bit the troopship sank lower and lower until her decks with the broken lead soldiery slowly became awash, and then, without a tremor, and blowing a fine jet of spume from some hole in her deck, she sank from sight.

Though we dragged for her where she had gone down, we never found the ship again. In the summer of the next year, when the pond almost dried up, I tried to find her without success. Evidently, when it had gone down, the submerged ship had slowly, under its weight of water, gone into the loose sediment mud way out in the pond, into which it gradually bedded down and, slowly covered by the mud brought into the pond by the following winter's floodwater from a nearby supply ditch, became covered completely. And so, hidden with its brave company of lead soldiers, the *Red Warrior* rested from the sight of the 'enemy' artillery that had sent it into the depths of the 'sea' between Mombanga and Zulu Mountain.

We sailed on this pond many types of craft between 1920 and 1923. Penny rowing-boats made of wood; a tin submarine, that I pierced a hole in so that it filled very slowly with water and then sank beneath the surface. It could be quickly hauled up again as it had a length of string attached to the stern. This afforded many hours of quiet fun. Then we made schooners, three-masted ones, whose adventures were many and varied. Sometimes they would be pirate slavers. At times vessels of the naval days of the early King Georges, or ships searching the coral islands of the Pacific for the hidden treasures of Captain Kidd or Black Morgan. These schooners were made from the white-painted fencing which fronted the farmyard of Appleby Grange. One of these pieces of fence, cut into three equal parts, made that number of excellent ships. One piece would be already pointed, forming the sharp prow, and the other two we cut away to points with a saw we always borrowed from Charlie Collins, a cripple, who got about on a short stool and who had a hand-propelled invalid's bicycle-chair to get him about the surrounding villages. By trade he was a boot and shoe repairer and he had taken over the first cottage in our row when he married Polly Austin, whose aged parent and brother had then gone to live over at Honey Farm. Each of these vessels would be fitted with three masts and fitted up with square cut paper sails made from either the *Daily Mail*, *Tit-Bits* or the *Kentish Express and Ashford News* (known to us locally as 'The Ashford'). So these white ships with their 'white' sails would be launched to sail in our youthful imagination to the isles of the far South Pacific and the Spanish Main.

Old beer bottles also formed part of our maritime stock-in-trade. These would be flung into the centre of the pond, unstoppered, and at them we hurled stones and pebbles until we broke them and they would be engulfed and sucked out of sight blowing spray and bubbles. Another apparatus we had was an old biscuit tin we had been given, complete with lid. This was a large tin, the same as used in grocers' shops for the sale of the biscuits. This became a giant submarine of cubic dimensions. Two holes were made in the bottom of it and, with a few lead soldiers put inside, it was pushed out into the pond where it slowly filled and gradually sank. A piece of cord was attached by a hole in the outside just below the lid by which we could haul the water-filled 'submarine' to shore and repeat the process.

One day we had caught some fieldmice and we used them as submariners in the biscuit tin. The lid was fixed down and the underwater vessel sailed out to the length of its cord and filled and slowly sank. Quickly we pulled the submarine up from its watery grave and into the bank. Opening the tin we found the mice still valiantly swimming inside. Suddenly the harsh croaking voice of old Mercy Fowle called out (she had evidently crept up on us unawares and had been, as we always reckoned, 'spying' on us). 'You wicked boys! I'll tell your fathers about ye, when they come home. You give they mice to me, my boys, if they beant a'ready dead,' said she. We handed over the exhausted and bedraggled mice and she took them back to her house, crying as she went, 'If they died, as sure as anything I'll tell yer fathers of your wicked ways!'

It was not until much later that day that the thought suddenly crossed my mind that maybe we had handed the mice over to an executioner! We the experimenters with deep-water craft had handed over the 'crew' to Old Merce who kept six cats within her home! Had we rescued them from the 'Three Mile Deep' in the 'Atlantic' to give them to Mercy to throw into the savage maws of her half-demented cats? That will always be a mystery.

It was in the Great Drought in the summer of 1921 when Garden Pond dried up, and we were able to explore its sun-ceamed bottom and find my 'ships' we had lost: old tins, with closed lids, rusting away with the red-coated Victorian soldiers mud-caked inside them. Many shattered bottles and a tiny silvery submarine we had lost in a sea-fight a year before: and a tattered sack, containing some rocks and the skeleton of a cat. How may years that had lain in the mud four feet below the surface of the pond we could not tell, but it had been immersed there for a long, long time as its condition testified. Putting an unwanted cat in a sack weighted with stones and throwing it into a pond was a favourite country way of killing a cat.

******

On the other side of the pond from our gardens was a square field we called Batt's Meadow. It sloped ever so gently away and was cut in two by a deep stream running north to south. In this stream grew the figwort with its peculiar flowers which always reminded me that they might have counterparts upon the Red Planet, Mars. In this field we played a great deal of cricket in the evening during summer, for the grass was almost lawn-like with stunted plants of the lesser knapweed growing here and there. When the Australians met England in Test Matches, then be sure we too had Test Matches, which we played strenuously in this meadow, with nut sticks for wickets, a rubber ball, and a bat shaped from a chestnut spike borrowed from one of Farmer Batt's hedges.

One series of these tests ended very excitingly. Both sides had won two games each, and fifth and last, the 'rubber' game was nearly at its close. 'Goldie' Goldup, from The Hollies near the Rose and Crown inn, was the last man in and batting soundly. The 'Australians' wanted one to tie, and two to win, as I delivered the last ball of my over. It was a 'Yorker' that I sent down, or a 'donkey-dropper' as we called them. It dropped some three feet in from of Goldie who swiped at it and missed. The ball rose high over his head and dropped right onto his wicket. He was out! We had won!

******

The deep stream crossing this meadow we had explored and had found many curious water plants besides the figwort. We surprised many fieldmice, a couple of water-rats and a pair of the uncommon water-shrews; also some moorhens and a solitary snipe. On the north side of this field a wide, shallow ditch carried overflow water from a sheet of water in an adjoining meadow. This was known as Clear Pond, for it was spring-fed and had never failed to have very large quantities of water in it however dry the summer. In this wide ditch I had tried to keep roach fish, but they disappeared overnight. There is little doubt that foraging moorhens from the ponds round about had caught them in the six-inch deep water.

Clear Pond was a peculiar place: it was surrounded with trees and spiky bushes and its surface almost covered over with grasses and weeds growing up and spreading over it. The water was a clear as crystal when scooped up in a jar, yet looked black in the shadow of the trees. It was really cold water and remained so even in summer. There was a sense of foreboding about this spring pond that even the warmth of summer days could not fully assuage away. It gave off an atmosphere such as one gets when reading the uncanny tales by Edgar Allan Poe. No fish lived in its sombre depths; no water-birds nested around its reedy margins. It was a pond, that to us, was a mystery, because it was so unlike the friendly ponds we had discovered and come to know, replete with happy memories of sunlit hours spent in and about them.

*And Nature, the old nurse, took*
*The child upon her knee*
*Saying, 'Here is a story-book*
*The Father has written for thee.*

*'Come wander with me,' she said,*
*'Into regions yet untrod,*
*And read what is still unread*
*In the manuscript of God.'*

*The Story Book*

# CHAPTER EIGHT

Not far down the road from the cottages, on the way to Greenhill, there stood a tall and stately ash tree over in Lost Pond Field. This was a favourite tree for climbing about in and hanging head downwards from its long, smooth upper branches. To be able to view the field below and the surrounding fields and habitations from an inverted position high in the air gave to me a feeling of such utter freedom that it cannot be adequately described. In its bole some twenty feet above ground, a pair of woodpeckers had their nests, year after year, unless at sometime a pair of thieving and bone-lazy starlings took possession of it to make a nest within for themselves. It was good to watch the green, scarlet-capped woodpeckers, or 'yafflers' as the folks hereabout called them, trying to evict the usurpers and chasing them with gaping bills to inflict summary punishment upon the flea-infested tuneless whistlers who were too tired to build a nest in a rotted tree, or in a barn or under the roof of a house or cottage.

Not far away lay an old-time farm called Brown's Kitchen House, in which at that time lived Mr Hills the wagonner at Greenhill Farm. Here too, with him, his wife and young daughter, lived his 'mate' who assisted him with his work on the farm. Brown's Kitchen House was just inside the Pluckley boundary and had small arch-like windows peculiar to all property on the lands of Sir Henry Dering. No new house was allowed to be erected on his estate unless it was made with these Dering windows. Evidently in the Cromwellian Wars between the Royalists and the Roundheads, a battle was fought at Pluckley by these contending parties and the local gentry and their followers were routed. One of the Derings was captured and locked up in a room which contained one of these small and very narrow windows. Being a slim man, this Dering was able to effect his escape from the Roundheads, and from that time this type of window has been a symbol of his outwitting his King's enemies.

Near to this old farmhouse was a huge barn, tile-covered; also the famous old hoppers' kitchen from which this house got its name in later years. The farm evidently belonged to a Farmer Brown: the adjacent hop-pickers' cooking-house nearby became fused into Brown's (Kitchen) House, and so it had remained named down to the times I lived near there. High up under the spacious eaves of the barn, dozens of house-sparrows built their nests in the spring. Inside, up aloft, under the dimness of the great roof we would go from nest to nest collecting their eggs to cook over our camp fire. When such of the eggs had begun to 'set', being advanced on the hatching stage, we left the nests alone. But, as soon as they were hatched and the young birds a few days old, the great brown rats which infested the barn would be up after the small sparrows and, dragging them from their warm feather-lined homes, would carry them off to their holes under the barn to eat in comfort.

The very old hoppers' kitchen was an eloquent memorial to those days of the good Queen Victoria when nearly all the fields and meadows hereabout were hop-gardens giving seasonal work to scores of local people as well as 'foreigners' from London, wandering gipsy tribes, and those untouchables of the roads, the 'pikeys'. These were not true gipsies, but wandering, homeless families who picked up work where they could and slept and lived in barns, under straw-ricks or beneath the hedges. Often they comprised a man who had picked up with a woman, both wanderers or tramps, and going together as a 'married' couple had children and tramped the roads and lanes all their lives long.

This kitchen was quite a large place, built of local ragstone with a tiled roof. The front was fully open and the interior was of good dimensions with an earth floor. At the back was the wide fireplace, where still hung chains with hooks, from iron bars set up inside the great chimney. From these hooks, suspended over roaring wood fires, the hop-pickers had in the long-ago days cooked their food in large iron cauldrons.

While I was at Mundy Bois, the old farm was condemned, for Father Strang at Greenhill did not think the expense of keeping it up was worthwhile. His wagonner, Mr Hills, grew wrath upon hearing this and got himself another situation in a distant parish. But his mate would not go with him and elected to stay with his employer, and so became a 'liver-in' at Greenhill Farm up on the hill. His name was Wakeman, and a nicer chap it would have been hard to find: a plump, ruddy-faced young man who had never a care, and always a civil word and jolly laugh for everyone. After the Hills had departed with ruffled feathers, the old house was securely locked up and left for time to tumble it to pieces.

Then came the summer of 1923, and Tibble-Mewden, the pet cat of Mrs Slaughter at Mundy Bois Farm, could not be found. This good lady, whose husband Captain Len Slaughter farmed, as a gentleman farmer, the large farm beyond the Mundy Bois crossroads, was distraught. The 'apple of her eye' had walked out on her, and was not to be found anywhere, and she, good lady, was not to be comforted. So she gave me the commission of trying to trace and find it, with the promise of a whole shilling as my reward if I could return her darling 'Tibble-Mewdies' to her awaiting bosom, a bosom which to my young eyes had always fascinated me with its ample, yet graceful curves.

During this case I was alternately 'Sherlock Holmes the famous detective' and 'Ned the Prairie Scout'. All my efforts came to nought. I even removed a small diamond of glass from the window serving the pantry in Brown's Kitchen House, so that I could unfasten the window-catch. Looking for Tibble-Mewdies at least gave me a pretty foolproof excuse to get inside the old house and explore it at my leisure. Yet the missing cat was not in there, strange to relate; neither was he up the great chimney. I reported my unsuccessful efforts to my employer. 'Keep a look out far still, won't you, Freddie?' she said, 'for someone may have stolen the darling!'

It was nearly the end of that summer when the small, deep, round pond named Road Pond tried up. This depression fed by floodwater was close by the road near to Brown's Kitchen House. Whenever a pond dried up its bottom was explored for anything exciting that might be found. Searching around I discovered a little heap of rocks of ragstone on the sloping side of the pond. They had not been there in the previous summer of 1922 when this pond had run dry. I removed them to find what might be underneath. To my surprised eyes was revealed the remains of a large black cat, all fur and bones, and around the neck of it a tiny collar. The skull of the cat was crushed in and its back appeared to have been hit in several places. Suddenly the thought flashed into my head: 'Is this Mrs Slaughter's cat?' I hurried up to the great old-fashioned farm, disturbing the Slaughters at dinner, the main repast of the day, held in the mid-evening by the local gentlefolks. I told of my discovery, and the good lady left the table and hurried down the road to the pond. I showed her the remains of the great black cat, and disengaged the small collar which she recognised. She was very brave. All she said was: 'The wickedness of it! But I'm glad you found Tibble-Mewdies, for now I do know what happened to him.'

Who had killed this good lady's pet? Who can ever know? Cats were the sworn enemies to nearly all who kept rabbits and chickens: they were the sworn foes of all the gamekeepers. Yet this killing was not a keeper's job, I was sure: they shot to kill, and kill quickly and hung them from their gibbets from which also hung other bird and animal offenders against their respective masters' game-preserves.

It was upon the barks of the willows around this pond that the bats would come to stay until the sun had gone fully down before beginning their evening flights in search of insects in the air. They were not the small black pipistrelles, but a large kind of reddish-brown bat, and I was able to study them at close quarters, a thing that the naturalist is seldom able to do. Only a good stone's throw from this pond was Willow Pond out in Lost Pond Field. It was flanked by willow trees along one side, and in the trunk of one of them Jack Luckhurst, who came from Little Mundy Bois Farm, and who was the special friend of my brother Walter, found the nest of an owl with an owlet in it. We wondered why he let out such a howl and fell down the tree. He had been pecked by the young owl who may have thought his questing fingers were some choice morsel brought in to it by one of its parents. Anyway, the owlet was taken out, being fully grown and a real nice little fellow, apart from its curved beak! I took it home to keep as a pet, and placed it in the attic where it could run about quite freely.

That same night, or rather early morning for it was around two o'clock, I was awakened by the sounds of footsteps coming down the attic stairs! 'Burglars?' I thought. Perhaps a ghost! The footsteps stopped. The attic door remained shut. Summoning up some sort of courage I got out of the bed, opened the attic door and there, sitting on the lower step, with its great unblinking eyes, was 'Jerry' the owlet. So I took him back again, closed the door, and retired. Five minutes later I heard him hopping down again, step by step. How many times I took him back I cannot recall, but I do know that this up-and-down-the-attic-stairs and door-closing awakened my mother, who soon put a stop to Jerry having a home in the attic. For all the house was awake by then. The next morning the owlet was returned to his old home in the nest in the willow tree. His large, seemingly reproachful eyes made it hard to part with him, but no doubt it was, Sydney Carton-like, a far, far better thing than I had done before in returning Jerry to his parents, wondering where their wandering-boy had got to the previous night.

******

Perhaps one of the happenings I remember most vividly was the night of the Great Storm. It was an early summer evening, the sun not long down, when I was passing the old barn near Brown's Kitchen. Inside I could hear movements, and now and then a cough. Wattle-gates had been placed together across the wide entrance to the barn and inside, filling its floor space to capacity, were scores of Farmer Strang's sheep ready for the sheep shearers on the morrow, when they would be let out two at a time to be divested of their thick fleeces. But they were restless, moving in and out among themselves, and sniffing at the air, and continually backing round hindquarters to the north. I watched them for a long time, until, far away came the roll of distant thunder. Looking towards Greenhill and across to Pluckley I saw the lightning flame over the sky, silhouetting Pluckley Church and its tall wood-shingled spire against the glare. Suddenly it had become pitch dark. A cold wind swept down from the ragstone escarpment stretching from Rock Hill at Egerton to Pluckley-on-the-hill. The first drops of rain fell, to a brilliant flash of aerial electricity, and almost immediately the thunder rolled like the war drums of the Gods of Old. Then the sky seemed to cave in and in five seconds I was half-drenched before I could gallop into the shelter of the old hoppers' kitchen across from the barn.

In the autumn and winter months Brown's Kitchen, which defined the surrounding area as well – the barn, the old pigsties, the kitchen and the three ponds – awoke to at least a week's activity when the corn and oats were to be threshed. Farmer Strang always gave his work of this nature to Mr Hooker of Egerton who lived over near to Newland Green. He was the engineer and threshing-man of his parish as Mr Dungate was at Kingsland over at Pluckley. Hooker's great steam-engines were to be seen all over the Kentish Weald during the threshing season, with their threshing-machines and caravans painted red. How those great old engines would thunder down the lanes, shaking cottages and farms to their foundations. How the children would rush out to watch these steaming monsters rumble by, to wave and should vociferously to the intrepid engine-drivers and their mates in their oily peaked caps. The fascination of those huge, treaded rear wheels and the smell of the smoke and the steam; the flashing fly wheel and the twirling balls of the regulator; the warm aroma of the heated oil; all these things cannot be really described, yet they can still be sensed in memory deep in the mind throughout life.

It was Mr George Collins who drove one of Mr Hooker's engines and he lived next-door-but-one to us. George Collins was always sent to thresh the Greenhill Farm crops, and every time the great engine rolled down the old Mundy Bois road towards Brown's Kitchen I would be out and following it. Always Farmer Strang would say to George Collins, 'Can you do with another hand, Mr Collins?' and would look at me standing by. After a bit of thought, George Collins would wink at the farmer and say, 'Sure-lye I could, if it were a good young-'un to keep an eye on the ingin and the cavings.' So I would be signed on at the princely sum of one shilling and sixpence per day, from seven a.m. to five p.m. with an hour's break for dinner.

Threshing, for I was at school some of this time, usually coincided with the latter part of our long summer holidays of six weeks. I would have many jobs to do, dear to my heart, like keeping a working pressure on the steam-gauge. 'Watch that red line on the glass and see that the needle don't git over it, nit under it, lad,' I was cautioned. Then there would be the water chamber to be kept topped up for the steam pressure, and the 'cavings' or chaff-sack to be watched, emptied and hung under the chaff ejector vent. And, best of all, the trips with the two large brown ale jars to the Rose and Crown which were filled for me to take back to the thirsty threshers, which included myself. When the ale was going the rounds, there I would be, with my own enamel mug for my share of ale and right well did I enjoy knocking it back with the best of 'em!

There is no doubt that Brown's Kitchen was a good central spot for the steading of the farmer's grain ready for threshing, and the great barn served a fine storage place also. Then there were the three ponds forming at their apex and corners a triangle inside which all the stacking and threshing was carried out, and they also supplied plenty of water for the great steam engine which simply gobbled up water when under working pressure. I have known, in a week of threshing, Willow Pond, Road Pond and Barn Pond sucked dry by this thirsty brute of steel and iron. When there was threshing under the way old Gipsy Wilson, who lived with one of his daughters over at Potter's Forstal, Egerton, would be with George Collins' team, who travelled all over Kent. I made good friends with this old man and he showed me many quick ways to put a man upon his back, slip out a gleaming blade and with a deft twist of the wrist, 'open his gizzard'. Having shown me such Boer Commando tricks as these I held him in very great respect, for he could be quick to anger.

It was always a great wonder to me how mice, still hiding in the corn and oat sheaves, would be fed, unwittingly, into the threshing-machine and go around the drums and through the rest of the machinery and end up, still alive, underneath the thresher with the seeds of weeds and other fine odds and ends, from which they would scurry like tiny grey shadows.

It was here in this area where we had, maybe, one safe retreat from the chase. How many times had Farmer Batt and Farmer Strang chased us into this place only to find we disappeared without trace? How old Mr Batt would swear as he suddenly lost us when we were almost in his grasp and within whacking distance of his stick. The old-time hoppers' kitchen was the clue to our fading from sight, for we would climb up its wide chimney until they had gone and then, peeping carefully out from the top of the chimney-stack, would watch them wend their incensed ways back to their farms.

*There's a whisper on the night-wind,*
*There's a star agleam to guide us,*
*And the wild is calling — calling*
*... Let us go.*

*Songs of a Sourdough* by Robert W. Service

# CHAPTER NINE

As soon as we arrived from Hawthorn Cottage, Pluckley, to take up residence at the centre cottage at Mundy Bois, I explored the house, then hurried out the back to have a look at our garden. It was a very long stretch of ground, though narrow. Such a strip of land is much easier to farm than a very wide place. Whoever had been in the house before us had never been very keen on gardening, for very little had been dug and cultivated. Almost all of it was grass, right down to the round pond we later named Garden Pond. We came to the cottage about a fortnight before Christmas 1919, and it being the 'dead' season of the year not much could be done to the ground at that time. Anyway, by the spring what had been dug was turned over, manured with horse-droppings I had collected in a bucket, cut and planted.

My father, who at that time was a long-serviceman; a Flight Sergeant in the Royal Air Force stationed at Ruislip (Uxbridge) in Middlesex, would come home for a long weekend leave once a month, and then every twelve weeks on a full week's leave. Smitten by the gardening bug he turned over a piece of ground following on after the planted bit, but as he was unused to such fork and spade work, he badly blistered the palms of his hands, and he never did any more gardening. Needless to say, I was pleased with the extra piece of tilled soil and soon got it planted up with potatoes. These my mother had purchased in the ordinary way from Lewis's Stores, up in Pluckley Street, and by judicious halving and quartering, I had enough 'potatoes' to plant twelve rows. The fruit side of my garden consisted of a large gooseberry bush and a clump of rhubarb.

During 1922 my Uncle Harry, who was out of work for a few weeks, was employed by my mother (his eldest sister) for a week to extend the garden for further cultivation by carrying on the tillage to halfway down the long strip of land. With all the old grass and earthy clods he built a 'dencher-fire' which, slowly burning internally, kept alight for two weeks, and burning gradually outwards left, when it had expired, a great heap of fine red earth dust which I sprinkled on the uncovered ground. I now had more land and was able to grow more potatoes (always King Edwards variety, for the heavy Weald clay suited them) and large quantities of greens, broccoli, cauliflowers, savoys, curly kale and one or two other varieties. Now that I had room for these vegetables, I was able to stop putting these in the early cultivated sections, and put in more broad beans, peas, lettuce, parsnips, beetroot and make a strawberry patch and a blackcurrant bush plantation. The lower half of the garden was left for grass, from which I got two harvests of hay a year that I kept in a miniature haystack as bedding for the two rabbits I kept in a large hutch secured upon stout posts to the side of the old outdoor lavatory that was near to the top of the garden.

Gardening can be full of adventures. The early preparation of the ground begins there; the waiting for the seeds to come up; the watch on seedlings and plants; the always-present fight against garden pests: the black and green aphids, snails, slugs, leather-jackets, centipedes and millipedes and the various fungi and moulds. The careful nursing of the less hardy vegetables in hot weather, and the continual weeding: above all, the battle against that fast-growing and tortuous rooted trailer and climber of the countryside – the *Convolvulus*.

It was on the grassy section of the garden where we had a bivouac camp in spring and summer called Grey Wolf Camp, a place of rest where under the tent, out of the hot sunshine, we could read in peace.

How well can I recall reading *The Boy Hunters* by Captain Mayne Reid under the shelter of the tent, stretched out full-length upon the warm earth and crushed, sweet-smelling grass.

During the winter of 1922, with a number of sacks found in the deserted and ruinous old mill near Pluckley, I made with some stout posts a hut in which we could spend a few hours during wet weather: for however bad the weather might be I detested being indoors, as did my good friends, Bob and Long John Beale. This hut had been in existence by a few days, when one rain-spilling night Mercy Fowle knocked upon our back door to inform us that the hut was afire! Quickly filling a bucket I sped to it and emptied the contents over the worst of the flames, beating out the rest with a stick. Surveying the damage the next morning, showed it to be a charred and ragged ruin. It was pulled down and no more permanent erections essayed. Who had set it alight? It had not caught fire itself, and we had not a camp-fire there that evening. Old Mercy told us that she had seen someone striking matches in the darkness down the garden, but she had thought it was us.

Shortly after the hut had suddenly gone up in flames, a shadowy figure had hurried away over towards the gardens of Mrs Hart and Mr Collins. Who had it been? Old Mercy Fowle and myself could only guess: yet the mysterious personage was always able to get away unseen, except for the running figure like a shadow Mercy had glimpsed just that one particular time. Mercy called him, for undoubtedly it was a him, for the shadowy figure had been that of a tallish man, 'That Sly Killer'. I always alluded to him – the unknown one – as 'The Invisible Raider'.

In after years, when compiling notes for this chronicle, I put two and two together. Now and again Miss Fowle would find one of her chickens killed by some heavy object, and left lying where it had fallen. Then there had been the blow that had killed my tamed wild cat Questie, for the cat had got home to us but in terrible agony and had died from a partly severed back. Then there had been the terrible tragedy of Tibble-Mewdies. All these things tied up; no doubt each incident could have been laid upon one man, seen but once, and then only a scurrying dark form.

******

Next to the cottages and their gardens, to the south, was a square field we later came to call 'Cuttie's' Meadow on account of it having been purchased by Mr Peter Cuthbert who built a long wooden bungalow upon it, and another section of it near the cottage being bought off Old Peter by his brother Charlie, who fenced it in and erected a small wooden bungalow not far off the road. In 1920, this field formed part of Appleby Grange Farm, owned at that time by a Major Woodcock, a Canadian, who eventually went back to Canada with his wife and little fair-haired daughters, who were always dressed in cream silk dresses and whose white overcoats were always trimmed with fluffy white fur. These little girls always gave me the idea that they had stepped right out of the Edwardian era into the hectic early post-war years of 1914-18. They presented a pretty sight, as did a nest of fully-fledge baby bluetits I disturbed in an old tree stump in Cuttie's Field that year, as they took wing and flew round and round my head like blue and white butterflies in the afternoon sunshine.

This meadow, being near the road and close to our homes, became a huge green playground for us. And there was a row of oak trees for climbing and upon the long bough of one (later incorporated with Charlie Cuthbert's piece of land) we had a fine long swing that sent us soaring high up and away, to return with a rush away back and high up to plunge dizzily down before the pendulum movements carried us again up towards the blue sky with its scattered white clouds. Sometimes young Vi Collins would honour us younger ones with her presence, accompanied by her friend Phyllis Batt, from Britcher Farm. 'Phyl' as Vi called her was as buxom a woman-like schoolgirl as was Violet, excepting her two long plaits of hair we boys called 'pig-tails'. So they would join in the fun and they would soar skywards, with their long, strong, shapely legs outstretched encased in black cotton stockings and showing above their tops as they sat flying through the rushing air, two or three inches of their gleaming white thighs. In this meadow of sporting memories we played Cowboys and Indians and such sports as cricket, football, rounders (with Vi always present); a peculiar game of golf with old walking sticks and a real golf ball, the property of Miss Violet, which we could never play with unless she played too! Then of course there was the swinging and the racing and the climbing up the thick rope tied in one of the oak trees; and a game I invented called 'Handball', a kind of football played with the hands and throwing the ball, instead of using the feet and kicking it. And there were us who 'played the game'; taking into the reckoning those who came and went in the hamlet between 1919 and when I left it in 1926: Vi Collins and Phyllis Batt; Harry and Jack Luckhurst; Jack Payne, Ashley Cuthbert and Goldie Goldup; Bob and John Beale and Ernest Blackman; his brothers Ted and Joe Blackman and my brothers Walter, Edward and myself.

\*\*\*\*\*\*

Just back from the road, and in front of the long line of oaks which stood upon a bank about four feet high, there was a stream that began at the south end and ran up to deepen and broaden out at the northern extremity. Here its waters gradually sank into the tough Wealden clay, and in summer it dried up as hard as a bone. Over the broader section was fixed a plank 'bridge'. In this stream we played and paddled and towed our 'schooner' on a string line across wide oceans and up undiscovered Amazonian rivers in our imaginations. With the coming of Mr Charlie Cuthbert and his bungalow in which lived besides himself his wife (who in some roundabout and complicated way, was distantly related to us through my Uncle George – who died on the Western Front in the 1914-18 war – having married the lady of his choice who was distantly related to Mrs Charlie) and frail-looking, yet very pretty little daughter called Joyce, or as her mother spoke of her, as 'her Joy-cee'; all this did not curtail our activities in our most popular old spot, now part of Charlie's land. We still had the broadest part of the stream and its plank bridge and the swing in the tree. Mrs Charlie, who was a keen naturalist, and my youthful self now became good friends, and I spent as much time in her home as I did in my own. She grew all kinds of plants indoors, as well as large jars full of aquatic underwater life, fish (such as stickle-backs and minnows) and tadpoles; added to this she had quite a comprehensive library (a rare thing among countryfolks), and two huge, wonderfully-illustrated volumes of Oliver Goldsmith's *The Story of the Earth and of Animated Nature*.

In the winter of 1922 my schooner became a 'lightship' and a permanent feature upon the broadish sheet of water below the bank upon which the Cuthberts' home stood. It was in harbour for the winter season, and its sails all furled and everything stored. Fore and aft it was anchored by real little anchors to the clay bed of the streams. Just forward of its main hatch amidships I had screwed an empty cocoa tin, punched with holes at its outer base, and without a lid. Into this was set half a candle and, when the darkness descended, I would light it, and the lightship gleamed in the dark and shone upon the water around it. Late at night, for the candle was never lit until near bedtime, I would get up and look out of our back bedroom window towards the Cuthberts' home some fifty yards away, and watch the light glowing on the ship in the blackness.

Then came a time when I purchased for a shilling a kit of parts with which I assembled a Sopwith, a biplane of Great War actions. It flew well, and when the wind was about right it made some fair flights. Then one day a gale sprang up; and on such a day a fighting plane like the Sopwith should go adventuring. And so it did; sometimes with the wind which whirled it aloft, and juggled it all over the sky until it plunged it to earth with a terrific crash; sometimes against the north-wester, which would hurl it backwards at astonishing speed and send it hurtling into hedge or tree. After an hour of such flying the gallant Sopwith was beyond repair. The next day I took it up into our back bedroom and, leaning out of the window, set fire to its tail and let it drop gently down to earth upon its last flight – shot down in flames! It pancaked below, and burned steadily out, until nothing but its grey charred remains were like a silhouette picture upon the ground. Contemplating it, I thought that many a burnt-our fighting plane must have looked just the same to pilots as they winged their way over the Western Front in 1918, a year but four short years away.

****** 

Cuttie's Meadow was the one place where we always celebrated November the Fifth. Here we would build up a high stack of brushwood, grasses and autumn leaves, and set up a 'Guy' with, as always, a pheasant's tail feather in its hat. The night preceding Guy Fawkes' Day we would black our faces with burnt corks, and with an old lantern tied on a pole we would go round our own particular district 'Guying', so as to collect money to purchase fireworks. We would sing the traditionally old refrain, taught us by our youngest uncle Harry Pile at each place we stopped:

> *Guy, Guy, Guy! Poke him in the eye!*
> *Hang him on a lamp-post,*
> *And there let him die!*
> *Holler, boys, holler! Let the bells ring!*
> *Holler, boys, holler! God save the King!*
> *Hurrah! Hurrah! Hurrah!*

For pronouncing this exceptional song at the top of our youthful voices we got repaid with anything from twopence to a sixpence.

Our wanderings took us from the cottages to the Cuthberts (these would bring in twopenny contributions to the total value of tenpence); then came Little Mundy Bois Farm, Appleby Grange (Scientific Poultry) Farms and Mundy Bois Farm (all sixpenny 'touches') then to the Weeks and the Glovers at the crossroads cottages (twopence from each); the Rose and Crown inn (sixpence); then to The Bungalows just past Mr 'Policeman' Goldup's house The Hollies, where we would collect three more twopences and then the long walk to Pluckley Pinnock and Pinnock Farm, where dear old Mrs Small would hand us sixpence, 'God bless thee' and say how it all reminded her of the good old times. We never called on old Farmer Stamford at his place across the way, for he had a snappish watchdog, a sharp-spoken ex-schoolmistress housekeeper, and knobbly walking-stick. Besides being a small farmer he was also an agent who collected rents for a lady who lived somewhere out in the vast Weald, and part of her far-flung properties being the Mundy Bois cottages in one of which I lived.

So our earnings, year in, year out, came to the usual annual total of four shillings and twopence, with which we were able to purchase quite a lot of assorted fireworks ranging from halfpenny Chinese Crackers to penny rockets, in Mrs Jennings' tuck-shop on Pluckley Hill, just where the village street commences. What a long time it seemed before it was dark enough to light the great bonfire. How the flames leaped and sprang about when it had been lit, and the ruddy fingers of flame curled around old Guy Fawkes. How we yelled when the supporting stake burned through and snapped, sending the flaming Guy headlong into the glowing embers. Then we would let off the fireworks, marvelling at their variety and colours and stars. Yet in all these occasions it seemed that at least one firework would be a 'dud' and tempted us to dabble with the God of Fire and Explosions.

One such incident happened to Ashley Cuthbert and I when we could not get a 'Jack-in-the-box' firework to go off at the end of a display in 1925, my last Guy Fawkes celebration at the hamlet. We undid the blue paper and coaxed out the powder; suddenly someone at the back – accusing fingers said it was Janet Cuthbert – threw a lighted match at the firework. It landed, still alight, right among the powder, which exploded the firework right under the very noses of Ashley and me. There was a great blue-yellow glare, and then darkness. I came to, and the world was upside-down. The stars in the night sky twinkled below me, and the dim outline of the hedge across the field was upside-down, too. 'Am I dead?' I thought. 'Is the world upside-down when one has been blown up and killed?' But gradually I came around, and so did Ashley. Our reflex action to the glare of the exploding powder had thrown us backwards, to end upside-down. And how everyone around us had a good laugh at Ashley and I the following day, when we emerged into its light: for the explosion had singed off our eyebrows, eyelashes, and quite a quantity of hair on the front of our scalps.

******

Lost Pond, a large sheet of water, situated in a deep and long depression or fold upon Greenhill, was a much resorted-to spot. Its margins were flanked with fine growths of reeds and rushes, and though no fish were to be found it had other compensations relative to natural history with its water-rats and voles, moorhens, coots and the rabbits that burrowed into the banks above the waterline. It was here, after reading how Nipper and Co., the St Franks schoolboys, had swum underwater with their eyes open in the South Seas, where they had gone with Lord Derrimore on his yacht in a tale running that summer of 1925 in the *Nelson Lee* weekly, that I made an underwater experiment to see if such could be true. Laying down upon the bank I immersed my head under the clear water of the pond and gingerly opened my eyes. Wonder of wonders! It was true! It was possible to open the eyes and see, yes, actually see under water. This opened up a new world to me, and when I wasn't holding my breath, with head immersed, watching water-creatures at Lost Pond, I was in my bedroom at home, with head below the water in our old metal hip-bath, searching out objects such as pebbles, upon its shining bottom, where I had dropped them willy-nilly.

******

Greenhill itself was an extensive hill, very high, and served by a steep and torturous narrow roadway. It extended into Pluckley parish to the east, Egerton in the west, and to Mundy Bois in the south. It is composed of large sloping fields, many of them red-covered; high grassy bluffs and rocky folds, and ragstone cliffs tangled at their bases with trees, bushes and the ubiquitous elderberry bushes. Upon its summit stands Greenhill Farm facing south, to look out across the great mysterious Kentish Weald, and beyond that the sea. What we called the Grassy Banks and the Rushy Fields of Greenhill became our wintertime playground when the sun was down. We would go sledging, or as some called it, tobogganing by the hour upon either the long-running lower slopes or the precipitous bank comprising its summit. On the latter sledging was an adventurous business, and more often than not, the sledge would encounter some hidden hummock or rock beneath the snow and the intrepid sledger would be either flung like an arrow ahead of the sledge, or would be left just sitting or sliding while the snow-vehicle raced and bounded on ahead! Then, after tea was over, one sledge, made from the back of an old push-cart or push-chair, the curved handles serving as the curved fronts of the runners, would be loaded with firewood, a cooking can, cocoa and sandwiches and, harnessing it up, we would pull it from the cottages down the road, along the old cart track to Mundy Bois Wood, and then branching off, climb the high slopes to the bluff and once atop of this, we had the snowy world to ourselves. It was good to be up there in the snow, with the wind whistling around one's ears, to gave out over the dim white world far below, beneath the night sky. Twinkling lights in the countryside below showed where habitations were upon that dim white blanket. We would light our fire and boil our cocoa. Then seated around the bright flames we would eat our sandwiches and partake of the brown beverage, imagining that we were Polar explorers of Captain Scott's Antarctic Expedition, in the earlier years of this century, and that we were high upon that great mountain of ice, the famous Beardmore Glacier.

Beyond Greenhill, linking Egerton village with that of Pluckley was the Top Road, from which one can see right across the Weald to the south, and as far as the North Downs to the north across the Charing Valley. It was through my friendship with Jack Reeves of Egerton that I joined the Egerton troop of Boy Scouts, becoming an assistant patrol leader after about three months. Our meetings were held in the coach shed in the stable yard of an old hostelry known as The George, perched right on the very summit of Egerton Hill, with extensive views of the Weald to be seen from its side windows.

I learned a great deal as a scout, and loved the pow-wows when our scoutmaster would tell us of his adventures with the Germans during the 1914-18 War. And yet, somehow, scouting had a certain amount of artificiality about it – or so it seemed to me. Perhaps it was because I had been a 'scout' in the years gone by: one of nature's scouts, a wanderer by field, wood and flood, finding out things for myself; getting first-hand knowledge of woodcraft and tracking, and camping and scouting under more rigorous and natural conditions than members of Scout troops can. How many had been the hours without food or drink when on some far-flung lone expedition into new country territory I had determined to live off this same countryside: maybe a few blackberries and bitter wild plums and a drink from a running stream. Or a few wild birds' eggs baked in a camp-fire and a few mouthfuls of 'bread-and-cheese', the small top leaves of the white hawthorn.

*So beautiful it is, I never saw*
*So great a beauty on these English fields,*
*Touched by the twilight's coming into awe*
*Ripe to the soul and rich with summer's yields.*

John Masefield

# CHAPTER TEN

The coming of springtime always meant to me the starting-point for new experiences and adventures. Our hamlet abounded with, in the warmer seasons, many grass snakes, and these snakes, unlike the venomous adder, are not poisonous. Many of the people around held them in dread, and the rest looked upon them with aversion, or as one might define, a 'mock dread'. Perhaps the most exciting and loathsome sight I have observed amongst the creatures of the animal kingdom was the coming across suddenly of a great writhing mass of grass snakes in a dry ditch under a hedge in a little squarish meadow below Britcher Farm. This meadow we called the Red Orchid Field for here grew, in early springtime, large quantities of a dwarf variety of the sweet-smelling purple orchid.

These snakes were evidently mating, and my cousin Jim Pile, who had come from Pluckley to spend that particular day with me, was along. We hastily drew out two old hedge stakes and set about that mass of reptiles with a frenzied good-will. How they writhed and scattered! How we clubbed and clubbed them, again and again, until we were able to count up our victims, eighteen in all, the others having escaped into the hedge to quickly vanish. We picked out the three largest and one of them, when we measured later, went exactly one yard from snout to tip of tail. We carried them back to the cottages, a fetid effluvia emanating from their bodies.

This was in 1922, and we were met by Mrs Collins, Mrs Ashdown, my mother, Mercy Fowle, and young Mrs Woodcock (from the end cottage) with cries of alarm and dismay. We were ordered to bring the reptiles no further than the gardens and to get rid of them. 'They're all sure dead!' we indignantly countered. 'No they be'ant!' cried old Mercy. 'They snakes will live until the sun goos a'down!' This was, of course, local superstition: yet a dead snake will continue to have nervous movements for a long time after its demise. With all the angry feminicians confronting us we had to give in. We could not keep them as trophies of the case: skinning them for their scaly coverings was also overruled, and so, very reluctantly, my cousin and I opened the old black-wood door over the nearby cesspool and flung them into the rotten black ooze inside, where they slowly sank out of sight, as had the villain into the morass at the conclusion to *Lorna Doone*.

In the Red Orchid Field in one corner was a grassy mound, oblong in shape, and some five feet high. This had always attracted my imagination. What was it? Who had made it? What did it contain? Maybe, I thought, the remains of a Viking chief, or a Roman general; or an ancient British chieftain, or perhaps some soldiers killed around this way in wars between the Cavaliers and the Roundheads. I asked questions about it, and the replies were of an unhappy variety, as they did not extend to such people as old warriors, treasure or trappings. Old Mercy said maybe it was made for hop-pickers to sit on and have their meals. Mr George Collins surmised it might have been a hillock flung up for the local gentry to partake of their luncheon upon, years ago, when there was a lot of partridge-driving and shooting going on around this way. Maybe they had set it up for old King Teddy (King Edward VII) before he was come to the throne, for he had been down, so he had heard, at the old late Sir Edward Dering's mansion, and gone partridging and pheasant-shooting with the parties from the Big House, as Surrenden was familiarly known. Old Mr Batt, who always had his weather-eye open for us, though after every chasing he let 'bygones be hasbeens' as we said, was approached about this subject. Pondering upon my query he at last said in language punctuated with cuss-words the following theory: 'Sure-lye that ... old heap has been there for long a'fore my time hereabouts. I expect that some poor ... hoss died here an' was a-berried under it. Maybe a few sheep a'died from some ... contagion, or maybe an old cow or two got a'struck by lightning or summat! Anyways I don't want ye boys a-muckin' around it, or a-diggin' of into it. If I a'catchers ye at it'll be the worst for ye young scamps!' Here he held up his gnarled old walking-stick. Such answers washed almost all imagination from my mind, though always a doubt lingered that perhaps something exciting lay inside.

Above this field, higher upon the slopes yet below Britcher Farm, grew a great pear-tree, entirely surrounded up to its top branches with tall hop-poles, legacy of times past, for now all this countryside was mostly pasturage for milk cows, where before the leafy, fragrant hop-gardens had held undisputed sway. We discovered in the side of this tree a cunningly-hidden door, made from hop-pole wood and so blending with the taller poles as to make everything look just as one. Opening, we went inside, and found that here all kinds of farming odds and ends had been placed. We named it the 'Britcher Lumber Room.'

Britcher Farm had been built in more recent times; red-bricked and with gleaming white paintwork and company's water supply. No doubt it commanded the site of some older farm or habitation, and could not have been more than forty years old in those days. A great sheepdog guarded it, and Alex Batt, a dour forthright man, old man Batt's eldest son, always cleared us off the farmyard if he saw us around. Later he emigrated to Canada, bought a farm, and was doing very well until his tractor fell over and killed him. Here also lived the other son, young Guy, who gave us cigarette cards from his packets of Players and Gold Flake. Over this lovely farm the good-looking and well-fleshed youngest daughter Phyllis held sway after she left school, taking over the domestic side. She had three sisters, two of whom had jobs away, Eva and Hilda, and Mrs Hart (who died, a widow, in 1923). All of the old farmer's daughters were lovely.

Mrs Batt had died when all her family was young, and it was Mrs Hart who had 'mothered' them until they had all, excepting Phyllis, left school. Now and again I was sent by Mrs Hart, who lived next door to us, on messages to her father's farm. This meant legitimate entrance. I would be asked into the great square living-room, all garnished and gleaming white paintwork and windowed all the way round. How everything shone, particularly the brasses and chinaware; how light, clean, sweet and airy was that room!

Above the farm was the large orchard modernly set out and at apple time a show place for all the finest eating apples one could wish to see: between these rows of short trees of champion fruits grew lines of luscious strawberries. We never got a chance to sample any of these fruits, for as soon as we were espied wending our way along the old pathway across the fields, a 'scent' in the shape of Guy or Alex Batt would keep an eye upon us until we left the limits of Britcher Farm, and came out upon the eastern parts of Rock Hill Farm, and then we became the worry of Major Gillespie, who owned that particular place.

Just inside the major's property hereabouts stood a giant beech tree, right on top of the high escarpment. This tree, the Egerton beech, was also known as the 'Lovers' Tree', for upon its smooth, grey, ample bole scores of names of courting couples were to be seen. Several generations had contributed towards these letters cut into the bark. Some, so old as to be indecipherable, and even older ones only made known by almost fully-healed scars. But the ardour of young love did not stay at arms' reach to carve that 'so-and-so loved someone else'.

The more audacious climbed the tree and carved initials upon the sides of the branches, and many a youth, daring to show his love was more than the others, had climbed forty or more feet up into this great beech to cut into its upper trunk that they loved true their respective minxes who waited coyly below.

******

Very often we would double-back from the Rock Hill land and 'Indian file' it back along the top of the escarpment to the eastern edge of Batt's prize orchard: yet our purpose was always defined. When we arrived there we found old 'Pecker' Brunger, who often worked at Britcher, 'a-keeping of a weather-eye upon ye!' Yet, outside of the fruit season the main attraction was exploring the trees below these long, high rocky cliffs, and the undergrowth which grew also over the face. Here, we hunted foxes, as far as it went. We would disturb them and, being so disturbed, they would give off a rotten-smelling effluvia that we followed, scenting like hounds until it petered out and, perhaps, if we were lucky, caught a glimpse of the fox as it vanished into thick, impenetrable underbrush.

About halfway along this cliff-like formation, near its base in a rocky fold, a pair of badgers had at one time had their lair until they had been dug out and shot. Years later, a lone fox had taken over this old badger's home for its own fox-hole. Just here we liked to camp, and always had a good camp-fire as there was plenty of old dry wood right to hand. The only trouble was that we could not cross the Batt orchard for a short cut to this spot, but had to enter the tangled mass at one end near Greenhill and force our way through the elder and whitethorn bushes growing from the base line to halfway up the rock-strewn slopes. Real Indian country, I always called it. Anyway, a day came when we had with us a long rope (an old clothes-line) and our way had taken us along the top edge of these ragstone cliffs. There Bob and Long John Beale and I suddenly stopped, attracted by the formation of the cliff's top, just at this spot. It curved inward in a rock fold. Laying down we perceived that below us was our camping ground by the fox-hole. Here was a short cut to this favourite spot. The rope gave us an idea. By tying the rope around an old stump near the edge, we could go down by the top to the camp-site twenty feet below. Then when we wished to leave, all we had to do was shin up the rope to the top.

Everything in theory does not always work out in practice. We soon found this out. The rope safely knotted about the stump, Long John essayed the first descent. Bob stood just back of the stump, while I stationed myself between the stump and the cliff's edge. Halfway down the weight of John upon the rope proved too much for this, what we had not realised, loosely-held stump. Pulling forward, it broke away and with it came about a ton of topsoil and rotted lumps of ragstone rocks. Before I could realise what was happening I was precipitated below, upon a disintegrating lump of the cliff. I glimpsed John land upon all fours below and turn his head in horror. I must have hit John as he rose up and sent him sprawling down the slope, myself following him, with the crashing thud of the earth and rocks in my ears just above me. The section of loosed cliff burst like a shell exploding, showering us with rocks and soil. One large piece caught Long John smack upon the back of his left hand, rendering it useless for some considerable time after. Bob, having been back of the stump, had got clear when it tore away. As John and I below, sorted ourselves out, searching for wounds, the cheerful voice of his younger brother floated down to us: 'I'll say you're a couple of silly...!'

There were times when Bob and John came down to my home that we would decide to adorn (though others might say inflict) our presence upon the village of Egerton, beyond Rock Hill. Our way would be by the old right-o'-way past Britcher Farm, to the Lover's Beech by Rock Hill Farm, crossing the Rock Hill Road down to a place called Toad's Hole and so burst upon Egerton just opposite Oliver's Garage. On our way, after we had left the giant beech tree, we would always stop to investigate a small though deep rock quarry to the right of the back way into Rock Hill Farm's farmyard. This ancient quarry had become, after many years, choked up by trees and bushes and a really choice tangle of briars. Here came many kinds of wild birds, such as chaffinches, yellowhammers, pied wagtails, and an occasional 'wind-hover' or sparrowhawk.

On one of these Egerton visits I noticed, many feet down in the right outer curve of this quarry, where the subsoil had settled and drifted over some vast period of time, a number of bones sticking out. It seemed impossible to get at them, yet they held us with their mysterious fascination. There was only one way to get them, and as I was the person who most desired these relics, I asked John and Bob to hold my ankles – 'and not to let go of them!' – and invert me over the side. I was lowered and held, upside-down, while I extracted the bones and studded them up into my jersey, which in this inverted position took the place of a sack. A long way below were the tops of quite tall trees growing up from the quarry floor, itself hidden from sight by the dense undergrowth. I shuddered slightly as I was hauled back, for a fall headfirst into that tangle, with no doubt scattered boulders of moss-covered ragstone rocks at the end of it all, might have proved fatal. Anyway, we had got our bones, which later, upon expert examination by an old shepherd, were proclaimed to be those of 'ship', the local dialect word for sheep. 'Been berried thar a moighty long toime, I should say,' said he. 'A real soight of a moighty long toime.'

When at such times as we descended upon Egerton by the old Mundy Bois-Rock Hill route we made our first call at our old friend Mr

Noakes' boot and shoe repair shop, perched upon a sixty-foot drop on the edge of the lower village street. Here we would swap gossip, of which we knew a-plenty, and help pass time away by perusing gory pages of illustrations in back numbers of the *Police News* that he took in regularly from Mr Moody, the newsagent at Charing four miles away to the north-east. Having given and received gossip, we would walk across to Mr Botting's general store and bakery to have a chat with him, and his son, and to minutely examine his latest wedding groups, local views and photos of social interest. Young Mr Botting was an expert photographer, and also a freelance man for many county and national daily newspapers. Some of his close-up work of insects, flowers, etc. I always contended were on a par with, if not exceeding in some cases, those of the famous professional nature photographers such as Eric Hosking, Richard Kearton (whose famous explorer brother Cherry I came to know in later years), W.S. Berridge, Francis Pitt, and George H. Vos.

Anyway, all his work was surveyed by eagle eyes, and if we knew any of the people in the group photographs they underwent a running commentary as to their appearances and pedigrees. Mr Oliver never allowed us near his garage, so we would go up to the top part of the village street on the flat brow of Egerton Hill to Mr Pile's large general store, which also boasted a post office. Mr Pile, a merry man at quip and jest, would parry and thrust at our badinage, and then, to show us that our further presence was not required, would tell us to pick, each, an apple from the apple barrel, '... and 'op it!'

Usually after one of these Egerton visits we would go homewards via the Top Road. From here one can look right away across the extensive lands of Court Lodge Farm, in a great tilled field of which an 'island' rises, capped with trees. This island had always intrigued us lads, and like the old mound in the Red Orchid Meadow of old Mr Batt, it conjured up all kinds of fascinating theories. A little way farther on, along the road, was Spanish Chestnut Spinney, and past that on the right, the narrow Greenhill lane swept away and down to Mundy Bois. From the top of this lane I had often stood and contemplated the high North Downs, three miles away as the crow flies, across the fertile Charing Valley. To the right was the smoke haze of Charing itself, and out in front, somewhere hidden in the dips and folds, were the villages of Charing Heath and its neighbour Lenham Heath. Here and there the North Downs bore white scars, legacies of old chalk-quarries, while at night in the winter, if the air was clear, could be discerned six hundred feet above sea level the lights in the big poultry houses at Roundwood Scientific Poultry Farm, the highest and most exposed chicken farm in Kent. After I had been left school some time, I was to find myself there, learning the intricacies of modern poultry culture, under Mr Cyril Biggs, and his brother Mr Gerald Biggs.

******

How eagerly we used to await the snowfalls each winter! It was at Pluckley, near to the village, upon the high gently sloping banks above Park Wood and the Old Ley (a fine sheep pasture), used as a landing-ground for aeroplanes of the Royal Flying Corps during the 1914-18 World War, where the real communal fun was to be had when the snow blanketed everything beneath its white mantle. Though we had sledging at Greenhill, and went on 'Polar' expeditions and camped in the high there, and also indulged in tracking wandering hares in the snow at night, following their spoor-marks for long and intricate distances, it was to the Mill Banks at Pluckley where we – Bob, John and myself – would go, as if drawn by a magnet, to mingle with our school-chums and the many grown-ups who would gather there, especially in the evening, when the snowy banks would resound to much laughter, chattering and hallooing, and lanterns would send their shafts of yellow lights spearing and dancing over the great whiteness. Below, Park Wood, a pheasant preserve of Sir Henry Dering's, would be transformed from a rolling area of dark trees and boughs to become a waste of sparkling whiteness, the trees and bushes festooned with frozen snow. Wandering through the woods and across the fields in mid-winter, with perhaps a foot of snow underfoot, and a windless grey sky overheard, the silent beauty and the latent terror of all this frozen vapour hit one hard enough to think upon, not only the beauty and the coldness of it, but also its numbing silence and its loneliness. Few people would be abroad in such weather out in the meadows and the woodlands, and even to sight Mr Small, of Pinnock Farm, spreading hay and dry pea and bean stalks for his flock of sheep, maybe a mile away across the vast white sheen of the Old Ley brought a feeling of warmth and kinship to the heart, and made the white-covered world seem a warmer and friendlier place.

But as I have remarked, it was on the Mill Bank, upon the round summit of which stood out, still black against its white background, the ancient mill of Pluckley, where we found the real fun and amusement of a communal character. As many as a dozen toboggans would be flying over the hard frozen surface of the snows at one time. There would be a continual coming and going of the tobogganists. It was here, one dinner time, that I had brought a can of hot tea from my home at Mundy Bois across the fields, to my sister Alice and younger brother Edward, who were at Pluckley School. This was in January 1923, I having left school the preceding August. We all had a cup apiece, and I then placed the can upon the snow near the old mill. I had a couple of sledge runs and then returned to get the tea-can, but could find it nowhere. My sister and brother had not moved it: no-one seemed to have noticed it. So I had another search, and finally discovered it two feet down in a shaft in the deep snow where it had warmed out a snug resting-place for itself!

Crashes were inevitable here upon the Mill Banks. Far beneath the covering of snow lurked many snags and pitfalls, in the shapes of scattered small ragstone rocks, frozen anthills, and tiny hollows and small ridges. From time to time, a single sledge would encounter something below the snowy covering, and its occupants would fly off into the awaiting drifts: or perhaps a toboggan, seating six happy passengers, would come to a dead stop, upend and fling the travellers far and wide, to roll over and over in the soft white flakes.

It was during the 1914-18 World War, when many men of the Canadian Expeditionary Forces had been billeted in Pluckley, that the 'Great Sledge' had been built. This large and very heavy toboggan, complete with thick iron runners, had been constructed by some of the Canadian soldiers to carry twelve passengers. Evidently the first time this sledge was used, full to capacity, it sped away at a terrifying speed to shoot the deep ditch in front of Park Wood and to cleave its way clear through the high, thick hedge, complete with its yelling load, to crash on, and career about until it hit an oak tree where the only remaining traveller, the steersman, got unseated and slapped against the unyielding trunk.

After this, a different and longer run was made: down the banks, through a gap in a hedge to the lower banks, and onward through a lower open gateway into Moorhen Meadow, where the giant toboggan ran itself to a standstill against the hedge of this field which separated it from the Old Ley. This was the second run of all-time at Pluckley. It was George Homewood, the Pluckley village butcher's son, who, upon his homemade sledge with detached frontal steering, made the record run for a small sledge in January 1923. He got his sledge as far, and just through the old gateway into Moorhen Meadow. He was a fearless tobogganist, and the most expert steersman I have ever seen. I was so fascinated whit his new type sledge that I begged for a run.

He let me have a go, and away I went. I guess I hit everything in that hazardous hundred-yard run! Ricks, anthills, the tiny dips and the small hard ridges; the remains of a rusty plough, some hidden brushwood, I found them all! When I was not speeding down, I was swinging around to face back the way I had been coming: I was flung left and right, backward and forward, yet by some miracle of instinct I still retained my position, though an ever-changing one, upon the rocketing, jig-jagging sledge. Suddenly the sledge and I encountered the tangled remains of a great stinging-nettle patch beneath the snow: everything became tangled up, and the sledge stopped, flinging me forward, to disappear head-first into the thick drift. Extricating myself, I came up panting, with something cold and bony around my right hand. It was the skull of an old farm horse! The horse had been left there the previous summer, after it had died, to rot away amidst the gigantic tangle of nettles.

*Pluckley was my playground*

*The explorer blazes the trail;*
*Others follow in his footsteps, so*
*The track is made and later*
*Will come the road.*

*Exploring* by Gilcraft

# CHAPTER ELEVEN

There is no doubt that the old windmill upon Pluckley Hill held a never-ending attraction to the Beale boys and myself. There it stood, topping what had become known as the Mill Banks, with its coating of black tar and its gleaming white wind-cap. There had been a time, many years before our family came back to Pluckley, that I could recall when this mill had four sails, or 'swips' as my grandfather called them. Somewhere, in the intervening years, a great storm had swept two of these sails away and piloted them down into Park Wood below the high banks: these swips were never replaced. This old mill had not been used for many years for grinding corn, though outside the former grinding stones stood against the lower brickwork which formed the cellar, or under-room of the mill.

Miller Buss, who lived on Pluckley Hill in the Mill House, opposite to Forge House, the home of Mr Wood the village blacksmith, had left the mill to itself after locking the entrance door. As time went by, the door was prised open and the old windmill became, from the storage room below ground to the wind-cap itself, a novel playground for the children of the village. Gradually, piece by piece, it was ransacked of all its portable articles by the villagers' children, among them, taken by John, Bob and I, a small iron stove that had helped to heat the office room in the windmill in cold or wet weather. This little stove we carried between us to Prebbles Hill Farm, where it was installed in the camp-house that Bob had built against the back of the old wood-lodge.

Pluckley Mill had the reputation of being haunted by a ghost dressed sometimes all in white and sometimes in complete black. It was on a winter's night in 1923 that Bob, John and myself set out late to visit the old place and try to see the ghost. Greatly daring we let ourselves into the mill and climbed from floor to floor until we reached the machinery room below the wind-cap. Emboldened by not having met a ghost we thought it would be a good idea to climb into the wind-cap and start the two sails revolving. It was Long John who always had to climb up into the wind-cap by way of wooden pegs let in the woodwork of the mill. From the trapdoor above he would then lend us two shorter-legged ones a hand to pull us up into the cap after him.

As John disappeared into the gloom above our heads, we heard a sound like a trapdoor being sprung. Suddenly the terrified voice of John cried out into the darkness: 'Help! Quick! The ghost has caught me by one hand!' Upon hearing this, and John's frenzied cries and kickings above, Bob and myself at once turned tail, breaking all speed records at getting from the top of the mill to the bottom and out the door into the open. We could still hear John calling high above, and calling us unprintable names! Suddenly we heard a great shout, and a heavy thump. By the time we had summoned up sufficient courage to return to the mill, John emerged into the night. Upon his right hand was a rat-trap, or clam-trap as we called them. 'Come on you two silly...!' he yelled. 'Help get this trap off me hand!' This we bravely did by depressing the spring.

Upon examining the trap we found it to be bound around the toothed jaws with soft rags, which saved John's hand from laceration and injury. Then we knew that the 'ghost' was this trap, and also knew that it had been placed up in the wind-cap to catch alive, and uninjured, one of the owls that visited the old windmill at night after mice, rats and beetles. This was the work of Dusty Buss, the old miller's son, who used such protected traps for catching owls that he would keep, tamed down a bit to sell to naturalists in Kent who required such birds.

During our many visits to the old windmill we had seen notices and pictures stuck down or tacked upon the walls of the room inside, as well as the many names written upon the weatherboards; and pencilled notes on uprights and beams. So I here append the following notes on the Old Pluckley Windmill, with the information written by millers of a Pluckley, past and gone into hazy memory. During the early 1930s the mill was hit by a thunderbolt, and completely destroyed by the resultant fire.

The history of the mill goes back from the 1930s for some two hundred years. This mill was not the original structure, but one built upon the site of the older one, from about 1820. One of Kent's best-known landmarks (on a par with the one at Cranbrook, the old capital of the Weald), it had not been in use for many years, until the winters of 1921-22 when Miller Buss had used it for sawing up log wood. The circular saw was worked by a revolving belt off one of the old wheeled shafts high up in the mill.

Perhaps the greatest enchantment emanating from the mill was when its sails were working, swinging noiselessly round and round, giving to one's senses the feeling of the uncanny. In the second room above the cellar, pencilled and penned entries upon the smooth uprights and boards were the names of former millers and their workmen: Buss, Stevens, Ashlee and Gotts.

But it is the following items that are of the greatest interest, forming some history of storms and damage, not only to Pluckley Mill but to others many miles away, and apart. Here are these records on the old woodwork:

*Brenzett Mill's sweep blown off October the 25th, 1865. Went through the roof
of a nearby house.*
*Lenham mill-cap blown off March the 12th 1856.* (This was written in
beautiful flowing hand and signed 'F. Swoffer, Miller, Pluckley.')
*Egerton Mill sweeps blown off during 1858.*
*Pluckley Mill painted white, 1891. Soon after had to be tarred.*
*Pluckley Mill struck with the lightning, August 16, 1831.*

In this second-storey room we also found an old illustrated almanack
for 1881 of J.H. & Son, a well-known firm, manufacturers of
millstones, at Newcastle. There was also a very ancient-looking
Valentine sheet, in colour, called the 'Family Musical Box', depicting a
military-looking gentleman holding a squawling baby in his arms!

******

Beale's Meadow, part of the farmland of Prebble's Hill Farm, was
composed of a high grassy tableland topping the steeply sloping banks
below which was the lower meadow, where, under the shelter of the
banks, and backed by large old fruit trees clustered the cowsheds,
chicken-houses and pigsties of the farm. Near the end of the lower
meadow which gave on to the Mill Banks and Mill Field, were two
ponds. One we called Weedy Pond, and the other, close by the edge of
Park Wood, was named Watercress Pond as it was full of this
succulent water-plant in its season. It was in the early part of the spring
of 1920, that I became friendly with the Beale boys, John and Bob, and
at that time we had another chum in our gang by the name of Percy
Sharp, who lived in one of the Prebbles Mill Cottages, on the summit
of Elvey Lane, not far from the Greystone house of old Mr Bishop, the
shepherd at Pevington Farm on the Top Road. Young Sharp we
nicknamed 'Blunt' because his name was just the opposite. He was a
much quicker lad than ourselves, and far less adventurous in nature,

yet he would follow us to a point, though often he would desist to our escapades and would leave us to find more agreeable companions more suitable to a quieter life and less hardy existence. It was one summer day, in 1920, when we had gathered at Weedy Pond, and had begun twisting water weeds around long sticks and dragging them forth to slosh around each other's unprotected heads and shoulders, when poor old Blunt, getting the worst of the weeds and the water, packed up and went off home, amid much ribald laughter on the part of we three boys.

Now and again, during summer days, we would get out the sledge from the farm, which held four of us at a pinch, and would go sledging down the very steep banks near the walnut tree that grew halfway down. The ground would be hard as iron, and the grass short, smooth and greeny-brown from the action of the sunshine. It was dangerous fun, for the sledge would gather a high speed in the passage of a very few feet owing to the extreme incline, and before one was hardly on the sledge one was at the bottom and flung rudely off it when it hit the meadow below, for the incline finished without any gentle sloping away. We got bumps, bruises and scratches galore, but it was exhilarating sport. Blunt would never indulge in these mad scampers, and perhaps, being timid, saved himself from harm.

It was after the Sharps moved away from the cottages that we found a tough and intrepid little chum. He was about our own ages, and very short, stocky, tough and without fear. It was 1923 when we finally abandoned this summertime sledging. The particular evening which ended these dangerous runs culminated in a bad accident to 'Tough Bill' Henniker, our new chum. We had been having single-seat runs down the bank and then decided to have a double-seater run. This proved very fast and finished with the occupants Bob and John standing on their heads and shoulders out in the meadow. The next run was a triple-seater with Bob, John and myself, and this proved even faster, with the sledge digging its stout nose into the ground and flinging us all in a piled heap several yards further on. Then came the four-seater run. Bill Henniker went up front, followed by Bob, John and myself. Away we went. The weight of the three in rear of Bill, as we rocketed down the slope, threw us forward, knocking him off the front of the sledge. The sledge careered downwards, passing over Bill as he rolled down the bank. We all ended up at the bottom: sledge, Bill and we three in a tangled pile-up. Bob, John and myself sorted ourselves out, pulled the sledge off Tough Bill and waited for him to get up. But he could not, for he had injured his thigh as he rolled beneath the laden sledge as it sped, top-weighted, down the incline. He was in great pain and, as he could not stand and our efforts to help him only increased his agony, we let him lie upon the warm soft grass. Passing along the meadow came the daughter of a bookmaker who had set up in business at Pluckley around this time, with 'Sweet' Smith from the ancient Kingsland Cottage not far away. They came over, and while the girl stayed with us, Sweet went to get help. He was soon back with a tall schoolfriend by the name of 'Ozzie' Rice, and two men from Kingsland Cottages. A hurdle, or 'wattle-gate', was procured from the Beales' cowshed and Tough Bill was gently placed thereon and taken along the field into the deep-cut land leading up to the road and then round to his own home. We explained the accident to his worried mother and father, and someone volunteered to cycle over to Charing, four miles away, to fetch Doctor Littledale. The next day, when I returned to Prebbles Hill, I was informed that the doctor had come around ten o'clock the previous night and had pronounced that our chum had torn muscles in his thigh and had been removed to the Ashford Cottage Hospital for necessary repairs. Eventually he returned home with a very bad limp and a walking-stick. For a good many weeks he hobbled about, slowly convalescing, yet he was left with a slight limp afterwards. To us three, Tough Bill was a true dry-eyed hero, and so he has always, in memory, remained.

******

There was always something doing in and around the Beales' farm, no doubt owing to the presence of our three selves. There was the time when Mr Beale had told us to keep away from the big cowshed, as the old brown cow, which was in calf, was a bit bad-tempered, or 'a mite mean and ornery' as the tall, raw-boned old farmer put it. Having been told to keep away, we, as was our custom in such matters, at once went down to the cowshed. Moving into the cowshed we espied the brown cow, and to our calls of 'Good old Daisy,' 'Nice old gal' and 'What's the matter my dear old brown cow?' she quickly showed us what was what. She lowered her head and charged: we fell out of the door in a heap, scrambled up almost beneath her hooves, and lit out for places distant and more friendly. Bob scrambled up the almost sheer face of the cliff-bank behind the shed to the plateau above; Long John, using his legs to advantage, with Daisy galloping after him, broke all speed records to get across the lower field, jump the ditch, vault the low hedge and disappear into the safety of the trees in Park Wood; I had run like some 'Tam-o-shanter' pursued by countless demons to reach the five-barred gate at the top of the meadow, where, on the other side, in the security of the deep-cut land, I was able to see John leap the low hedge, and young Bob make his final scrambling effort to the top of the cliff-bank.

It was upon the great field atop the high banks at Prebbles Hill Farm where we would play occasional games of football and cricket, and indulge in running matches and any bit of sport or fun that happened along. In the spring of 1920, I recall two very vivid things, one of them being an unexpected flight which Blunt Sharp, Long John, Bob and I went upon. We had found a large tarpaulin at the farm and we took it out into the high meadow to play with it. At the time a gale wind was blowing and as each of us held a corner of the tarpaulin the wind filled and bellied out the waterproof sheeting and pulled and tossed us hither and thither over the grass until, all of a sudden, an extra strong blast caught the tarpaulin as it was more or less flat upon the ground, yet one end being held by two of us a couple of feet higher than the opposite side. The wind swirled underneath, billowed it out and drove it almost directly upwards into the air. It happened so quickly that we were nearly twenty feet up, each hanging onto his respective corner, the meadow flying away beneath us. Then some of the pressured air spilled out, and old Blunt let go at about ten feet above ground. This made his unattended corner rocket up, spilling the rest of the air; the tarpaulin like a torn parachute collapsed and we three others plummeted from the higher level, now about fifteen feet to the earth beneath the tarpaulin, falling after and upon us, covering us like a shroud. We gathered ourselves up, miraculously uninjured. This pioneer, primitive flight was far more exciting when, in 1927, I had my first aeroplane trip in an Aero-Avian biplane, with open cockpit, a board for a seat, no safety strap or parachute, and the slipstream from the propeller such a solid lump of velocity that I had to really force myself into it to enable me to view the ground hundreds of feet below.

It was in this field that in that spring of 1920 I first had my more or less innocent sense fully sprung to that most natural of events, reproduction and birth. It was nearing the end of the lambing season, and I was with Bob and John at the farm while they had a hurried dinner before we disappeared into the countryside until tea-time. Getting over the stile from the garden into the top field I saw, under the hedge, a sheep with its lamb newly born that morning. The old sheep was busily licking the vestiges of blood from the fleece of the wobbly-legged, bleating little fellow. Under the hedge, not far away, was further horrific-looking evidence of the birth of this lamb. I turned to John and Bob and asked about the blood on the lamb. Bob, who was only nine years old at the time, assumed the air of an expert on such matters to remark: 'All lambs have blood on 'em when they are born!' 'Why?' I wanted to know. 'Because,' says Bob, 'they comes out of there' (indicating the rear anatomy of the mother sheep) 'and the old sheeps bleed a mighty lot, but they soon gets over it!' This was all very sudden, rude and crude, knowledge; yet I had the intelligence and most certainly the vivid imagination to grasp at once, that everything that bears alive into the world its young, does so in pain and suffering. From that day onwards I held all mothers in deep respect and marvelled at their spirit and fortitude.

In this field we played our Cup Final each year: Red Rovers versus Kingsland. We could not, apart from a proper school team, gather together twenty-two players to form two opposing sides, so we did our best. This annual Cup Final was held at Beale's Meadow, in the Aprils of 1921, 1922 and 1923. The Red Rovers team (representing the hamlet of Mundy Bois) was made up of myself as the goalkeeper; my brother Edward, who was only six years old in the April of 1921, played back, certainly only in name! Bob Beale was centre-forward and Percy Sharp (and later Bill Henniker) played any other forward position he so desired. Kingsland was made up from 'Toddy' Todd in goal; his step-brother 'Smudger' Smith centre-forward, and Don Black as a back and his brother Jack as another interchangeable forward. The Black boys lived at the house of their grandfather, Mr Dungate, further along Top Road. At the back of Mr Dungate's place was a great yard where he kept his great steam-driven tractor engines, threshing-machines, travelling caravans and other paraphernalia of the threshing world. Here too, were his engineering workshops, and gleaming machinery protected by wire cages. And at the back were the Kingsland oast-houses where hops were dried, but these belonged to Sir Henry Dering. The white cowls upon these oast-houses each had a weather-vane sticking out, upon the surfaces of which the prevailing winds turned the cowls so that the smoke and fumes from the drying kilns below could be blown away from the oasts. Each vane was surmounted by a rampant white horse, the insignia of the county of Kent.

The last Cup Final in April 1923 was a very exciting game indeed, the Red Rovers winning by a goal to nothing, the winning and only goal being scored by Bob Beale in the very last minute of this great game. Here are the names of we who played in that last Cup Final in the Top Meadow at Prebbles Hill Farm in the year 1923:

*Red Rovers (Mundy Bois)*
Goalkeeper, F.W.T. Sanders
Full back, John Beale
Centre-forward, R. Beale
Outside-right, W. Henniker

*Kingsland United (Kingsland)*
Goalkeeper, Donald Black
Full back, Toddy Todd
Centre-forward, Smudger Smith
Outside-right, Jack Black

\*\*\*\*\*\*

Everything around Prebbles Hill Farm had some use or interest for us three. There was the old buck rabbit that John used for breeding purposes for his three doe-rabbits. This bad-tempered old fellow had often savaged him, and he bore many long scars upon the back of his hands where the buck had nipped them open with the hard nails of his fore-paws. This dour old rabbit would even set about Tommie, young Bob's cat, and make it turn tail, only too glad to get beyond the tearing paws of the 'Old Devil' as Long John called him. The cat was our great favourite, and would follow us for long distances, until it grew tired of our company, when it would wander away back home. Another pet of Bob's was his white pigeon, called Percy or 'Perce'. This bird would follow him upon the ground, or fly after him, often setting upon his head or one of his shoulders, and staying put even while Bob wandered around, chopped wood, cleaned rabbit hutches out or did other odd jobs around the farm. Some other 'pets' he kept in large preserve jars, filled with water. They were fed on brown sugar, and manufactured a fluid which turned the water to a clear deep brown colour. This liquid was known as 'Bee-wine' and was not at all bad to drink. These 'bees' as far as I could gather were yeasts which turned the sugar into secretions which became infused into the water turning it to wine. These yeasts would rise and sink in the liquid and gave the impression of having animal life. Old Mr Beale, when he was us from time to time imbibing this wine, would remark: 'Sure as anything, you boys'll be a-pizening an' terselves 'fore long, mark what I say!'

In their seasons in the front and back garden of the farm would be fine plums, great sour gooseberries and crisp redcurrants for us to gorge ourselves with. It was behind one of the huge gooseberry bushes where we had a secret entrance into a part of the gnarled elder hedge. The hedge-bottom, once one got into it, was quite clean and dry, about four feet wide and clear to a height of about three feet. Here we would crawl, if any quite local trouble took place, and remain curled up, aware of all that was going on outside, yet cut free from the fear of detection from without. Hence we disappeared when some prank had roused Mr Beale's ire, and he would be looking for us to 'stick' us with a cane. Under the friendly shelter of this elder hedge we also hid from an irate Mr Bishop, from time to time, the old shepherd at Pevington Farm. He always wore an engine-driver's glossy-peaked cap, and what with our raids upon the Pevington cherry orchard, and our calling after him 'Wot my old Captain!', 'Good day to you, Admiral', and 'How's Sir Francis Drake, this morning?' his temper would be raised very high indeed and he would lumber after us, shouting 'Sarcy young varmints, I'll have your gizzards out!' and shaking his stout rod of wood at us, endeavoured to catch and chastise us. Not far from Elder Hedge Hideout was the camp of the Beales. It was a sort of roofed lean-to against the field side of the large wood and toolshed of the farm. It was a roomy camp inside, being built from hurdles, sacks and a large tarpaulin to keep off the weather.

It was fully enclosed and had a small open door at one end. In here we had the little iron fire-stone we had 'captured' from the ruinous mill at Pluckley. In this camp, around the glowing stove, during the long cold winter evenings, we gathered to exchange gossip, swap yarns, sing songs and eat stew from the old iron pot upon the stove. And what stews they were, made from potatoes, cabbages, cauliflowers, onions, carrots, turnips, rabbit meat and plump house sparrows! This was an 'open camp', not a secret one like so many of our strung-out fortifications from Pluckley village to Smarden Forest. Here would come our school-chums, to chat and yarn and partake of whatever rough refreshment might be on the 'menu'. The following, at various times, would visit Beales Camp, when we three were 'At Home' to visitors: there would be 'Sandy' Turner, son of the village builder and undertaker; George Homewood, son of the Pluckley butcher; Oswald ('Ozzie') Rice, from Kingsland, and also from that part, Jack and Don Black, Toddy Todd, and his step-brothers Sweet Smith and Smudger Smith. Then there was Bill Henniker and Percy Sharp of Prebbles Hill cottages, and sometimes Walter Buss or his younger brother Hubert from Elvey Farm below the high escarpment. Once in a while Willie Croucher from Pluckley Hill would pop in, or perhaps the Gore boy from near Pevington Farm (known as Pevington House also) of which farm his father was bailiff. Once in a while young Miss Bishop, Alice to us, the youngest daughter of Mr Bishop the shepherd, would honour us with her presence. She would peep in the door, say 'Hello! What you cooking in that pot?', have a look at it, turn up her nose and walk out again to the exclamation of 'Gracious!' We could almost hear her, when she got home, confiding to her horrified mother and invalid elder sister 'My oh my! Mother, I'm sure those three boys are stewing frogs in their stew-pot!'

******

Secret Camp, which later became known as The Fort, was situated upon the steep side of the ragstone escarpment not far from the farm of the Beales. The ledge upon which the camp was built was well over halfway up the rocky face, being about ten yards long, six feet wide and overhung with the outcropping of rock and subsoil above so as to form a roof impervious to all weathers. Upon the subsoil grew trees, bushes and grasses: sloping away from the edge of the ledge a steep, loose-soiled, rock-strewn embankment went down to the tilled land some thirty feet below. From its base up to the ledge it was crossed with tall elder bushes and trees and, especially in springtime and summer, the foliage screened the camp from anyone below. A short, steep, winding path, with small flagstones put there by some forgotten generation, led down to the ledge from the cultivated field above the escarpments. No-one knew of this really forgotten path and secret entrance near the old holly upon the high ground. This camp was our best and finest. A real secret retreat, dry, roomy and comfortable, not far from the farm and within not too far 'raiding' distance of orchards and Pluckley village itself.

From here all approaches could be watched, and from the top of the ancient holly-tree above every point of the compass was covered. From this observation point we could view Prebbles Hill, Pevington Farm, right across to Nettle-pole Lane at Little Chart and as far as the North Downs three miles away above Charing. To the south the view included the vast, wooded Weald, all the land out Smarden way, and Pluckley Thorne and the Pinnock lands. East was Park Wood, the mill banks, and Pluckley village, as well as Kingsland. The old tree was known as Holly Tree Lookout, and the top was composed of spikeless leaves, though those upon its lower branches were very prickly. No doubt this had been caused by botanical evolution to stop cattle from earing the lower foliage, the higher branches being beyond reach, not being spiny. Upon the flat-lined top of this tree we built a wooden platform upon which we could sit in comfort and spy upon everything and everybody for far distances without ourselves being seen. We raised a flagstaff atop of the holly tree and for this I designed our battle-flag. The design was in fast light blue set upon a white background. The flag I cut from a piece of old sheet, and it measured six feet by three. How proud we became of our flag, especially myself, for in my goings and comings on schooldays in the field below, I could gaze at it as it flew, unfurled to the breezes, two hundred feet above the levels below it. The design was made up of a cross, quartering it. In one quarter was drawn an eagle; in another an unsheathed sword; while the two other quarters had between them a lion and shield with crossed spears aback of it.

\*\*\*\*\*\*

It was in 1924 when wireless came to Pluckley. The first receiving-set was a crystal set made by Ozzie Rice's much elder brother at their home at Kingsland cottages: the end one to the old stone cottage in which the Smiths resided. Soon all the village knew about this wonder and people from far and near came to visit the house in the evenings to try on the headphones and 'listen in' to the latest miracle of the Modern Age. As soon as Bob Beale and myself heard about this and had inspected the mast and aerial of Ozzie's brothers, we made a 'wireless' set for our own particular use. We raised a mast near the flagstaff on the holly tree, complete with aerial and wire. The wire went from the tree high over the old deep-cut lane to the tall trees flanking the western side of the farm's large back garden. From there it was relayed down to the Beales' Camp. With one of us on watch and by a prearranged code of signals, the 'lookout man' could tap upon the aerial and transmit messages to the homemade 'headphones' inside the camp. The messages were in numbered tappings: one tap at two-second intervals if Farmer Jesse Buss and his son Walter were around or his workmen 'Plushey' Austen, 'Grandad' Austen or Doddie Smith; double taps for Mr Gore, his son, or 'Admiral-Captain' Bishop, from Pevington Farm; triple taps for Mr Beale (if he happened to be on the warpath); quadrupled taps for the Kingsland gang, and succession of rapid taps if a gamekeeper seemed too interested in our locality.

Perhaps some of our happiest moments, outside of rioting about and general mischief, were those on summer evenings when we would sit around the flaming camp fire on the elevated ledge of The Fort. There would be Bob, John and I, with maybe (in his time) Blunt Sharp, Bill Henniker, the 'black' Smiths and the Black boys themselves. Many and varied were the songs and ditties; across the fields would float our youthful voices as we sang 'There's a long trail a-winding', 'Carry me back to dear old Blighty', 'Where do flies go in the wintertime?', 'That

Coal Black Mammy of Mine', 'Goodbye Rachel', 'Pasadena', 'Horsey Keep Your Tail Up', and that riot 'When Father Papered the Parlour' and many, many more. We usually ended by singing two or three times over 'Where are the Boys of the Old Brigade', a rousing song taught us by Mr Turff in school at Pluckley, the headmaster beating out the notes upon the school's ancient harmonium.

And there were other songs that he had not taught us, and which, no doubt, would have brought a very shocked look to the tranquil visage of dear old Canon Springett DD, our rector, such as a revised version of 'Sweet Violets' and some ditties that had been spondered outside of the normal world of music such as 'We were Down the Sewer' or 'As Eve Said to Adam', sung to tunes to be found in *Hymns Ancient and Modern*.

There came a time, in the summer of 1923, when the Kingslanders declared battle upon us at Secret Camp (The Fort). Our escapades had annoyed so many folks around, that the Smith boys and the Black boys crusaded against us to overthrow our rule, capture Secret Camp and haul down its flag. On their way to do battle with us they roped in Toddy Todd and a young Buss boy who lived at Pluckley north crossroads, named the Turnpike. It was six against three, for Bill Henniker was *hors de combat* at that time, and we were thus outnumbered two to one. Smudger Smith led the attack from below, telling his 'troops' to chuck clods of earth and stones upon us on the high ledge, though we were well screened by the elder bushes on the top part of the high slope. He attempted to rush us, under covering fire, by climbing the slope and attacking us with his fists and a hedge stake until the covering troops could follow him and reach the ledge. But Smudger met with such a heavy fire of hard clods of earth that he turned, tripped over and crashed through the pithy-stemmed elder bushes to the field below. Then, licking his wounds, he ranged his 'army' at intervals along the lower part of the slope and got them to keep up a terrific fusillade of small rocks. They showered around us, and we had to lay flat near the edge of the ledge behind the screen of bushes and hold our own fire. There was only one thing for us to: we waited until a break came, while they piled ammunition, then we attacked them! Gathering as many large stones as we could we stood up and with a well-worn battle cry we rushed down the steep slope, crashing through the elder bushes to emerge facing them at about twenty paces. Caught unawares they had no time to do anything, for we pelted them with stones as fast as possible. Under the shower of lumps of ragstone they broke, and ran for the five-barred gate into Beale's lower field. Only Smudger stood his ground, calling to his men to 'come back you bloody lot of cowards!'. Hit hip and thigh with stones, he gave ground and dashed for the gate and the field beyond. We followed, packing as much ammunition as we could and chasing them back towards Kingsland. They continued to retreat and we had won the Battle of Secret Camp. It was never assailed again.

*I once knew all the birds that came*
*And nested in our orchard trees;*
*For every flower I had a name,*
*My friends were woodchucks, toads and bees.*
*I knew where thrived in yonder glen*
*What plants would soothe a stone-bruised toe...*

*Oh, I was very learned then,*
*But that was very long ago.*

'Long Ago' by Eugene Field

# CHAPTER TWELVE

To go exploring always meant adventure, and that is why, either personally of with the help of John and Bob, exploration work so often figures in our weekend programmes. The exploration of the Elvey Escarpment was one of these. One very warm and sunny early summer morning in 1921 we three set off from Secret Camp (The Fort) to explore these inland cliffs and their jungle-like lower slopes. A rocky trail led from this camp to peter out just inside the borders of the 'jungle' through which we had, in many places, to hack our way with an old handbill or wood-cutting chopper. This mass of riotous vegetation, consisting of fully-grown trees, close-growing clumps of elderberry bushes, prickly whitethorn, and six-foot-high growth of stinging-nettles and thistles, ended where the ground became cleared where some hundred yards of the escarpment had crashed down at some period beyond living memory; though the very old people always referred to it as the 'Pluckley Landslide' and it had possibly occurred in the youth of their parents or in the times of the latters' parents. It is quite possible that this landslide took place during the 1790s.

Cutting off the great ley-farming lands of Farmer Buss from his large Top Field above the escarpment, grew a stretch of high whitethorn known by us as Whitethorn Thicket. Here, in springtime, grew thousands of wild white violets. There was only one way in which they could be obtained – for we collected them to sell to the gentry in the village, and at Mundy Bois – which was to crawl belly-flat over the broken earth and rock rubble where there was a clearance of about nine inches from the ground to the lowest interlacing branches of the bushes with their numerous sharp spikes. It was easier to get in than to back out and we usually ended up with smarting backsides from the lowest thorns, for there was always the instinctive movement to lift the knees to work back, so raising the posterior; one could drag forwards quite flat by elbow action with the added advantage of seeing ahead. As the jovial Bob would so often remark, 'One needs eyes in their backside to get out of such places!'

It was here where the landslide had occurred that I first found evidence of the fossil shellfish of upper greensand or ragstone formation. Of these shells, of the form of *Terebratula*, I made quite a useful collection. Many happy hours I spent there below that thicket, chipping out these fossils with the help of an old hammer. Knowledge of rocks, crystals and fossil remains was hard to come by, as the village was happily content not to be able to boast of such information. It was not until Mr and Mrs Charlie Cuthbert came to Mundy Bois that I was able, through two large tomes of Oliver Goldsmith's *A History of the Earth and Animated Nature*, to obtain real facts upon earth-lore. How useful would have been to me, in those early days of questing after knowledge, such books as I was able to buy in much later years, as Mantell's *Medals of Creaton*, Geikies' *Geology*, Buckland's *Geology* in the Bridgewater Treaties series, Lyell's *Students' Elements of Geology* and J.E. Taylor's *Our Common British Fossils*!

Beyond the thicket one again entered the lower slope of the further section of these cliffs. Here was a well-defined trail leading through the jumble of great nettles and elder bushes; a trail used frequently by we three, rabbits, badgers and the red foxes. This ended where the slopes finished to verge with the ley-farmland, leaving the cliff-like formation of ragstone towering above us, to give the trees aspect of what the whole range of this escarpment must have looked like some hundred and fifty years before.

******

Now and again, in the ploughing season, we would 'help' Doddie Smith, who worked for Farmer Buss of Elvey, to plough the Top Field above the high ground. It was a tricky field with little real subsoil but plenty of rock rubble. Over and over again the print of the shining plough would suddenly go deep through a patch of this loose stuff to throw over the plough and drag the two horses to a halt. Hidden beneath the surface were many large rocks into which the plough would run its nose, like a ship fouling a rock beneath the surface of the sea. Then it would, against the resistance, be up-ended and thrown upside-down. There had been one spot in this field where the horses had plunged in up to their bellies and the plough and ploughman disappeared almost from sight in a cave-like depression. Yes, it had always been dangerous work to till that rough Top Field, and in our days only Doddie Smith, 'helped' by the Beales and myself, essayed to do it; we boys with much scampering, cavorting, loud calls and cries, and Doddie serious-faced and very determined to get it done as soon as possible. 'Why do you plough it?' we would ask him, and he would reply 'Because I ain't the boss!' A good enough reply for us.

It was in this Top Field where Bob and John found the nest of a corncrake with ten eggs in it. I kept one for my collection, the others being left in the nest to hatch. We never saw the birds themselves, and it was not until the summer of 1923 (the eggs having been discovered the previous summer) that I was able to identify them as those of the corncrake, from a little shilling book I purchased in Ashford called *Birds and their Nests and Eggs, and how to identify them* by W. Gallichan.

In this high tilled field we could always come upon pheasants and partridges' nests and from the eggs not 'set' (with embryo chicks in them) we could partake of our favourite feast: fried game-birds' eggs!

How many times we were chased by Walter Buss the farmer's eldest son; how many avoiding actions we had to take from Surrenden's gamekeeper and Police-Constables Smith of Egerton and Legge of Pluckley upon their following-up of 'information received'!

It was on the borders of this field, opposite to where old Captain Bishop's cottage stood, where I met my Waterloo, which kept me out of action for six weeks, the day after I left school in August 1922. Across the lane from the shepherd's cottage grew a bullice-tree, bearing at that time of year a lovely sweet, golden, plum-like fruit. These bullices I had a great liking for, and as these trees were few and far between, those known were mind-indexed for future use. The only other bullice tree was in the corner, near the road, of old Rose Marchant's garden near the Fir Toll on the way from Pluckley village to the railway station near to the Pluckley Brick and Tile works.

About nine o'clock of the morning just mentioned, on my way to visit the Beales, I stopped off to climb the bullice tree and gather some of its fruit. I had barely got well into the tree when I noticed Farmer Buss and his son Walter and two of their men out in Top Field. Walter spotted me in the tree just as I perceived him. He called out for me to get down, and came running across to it. Quickly, too quickly, I turned to descend, slipping off a main branch as I did so. Down I fell, only to be brought up with a terrific jerk to find myself suspended in mid-air, a three-inch sprog from the tree having caught me underneath my left armpit.

There I hung, shouting to the Beales and Blunt Sharp who I could see atop of the holly tree in the clifftop above The Fort. They were too far-off to translate my cries asking for their help. They called back and waved and pointed out to me the fast-approaching Walter, who was coming from across the pea field. Grasping a higher branch I eased my arm off the sprog, a broken short branch, and then dropped to the ground. Seeing me out of the tree Walter Buss, evidently with farming honour satisfied, went back to help the others harvest the field peas being cut with old-fashioned sickles. I could feel blood squelching under my arm, and I divested myself of my blue guernsey, and, opening the front of my shirt, peered under my arm. There I saw the extent of the damage. As I had fallen the sprog had caught my fall and had torn the skin and flesh from the underarm for several inches, of about an inch in width, rolling it neatly, or perhaps rucking it up.

I could see it meant a surgical job. There was no pain, only a smarting throbbing, and the blood had ceased to flow. Evidently my cries for help had been heard from the Bishops' cottage, and I had been seen hanging from the tree by the eldest Miss Bishop from her bedroom where she, as a victim of leg-bone tuberculosis, spent most of her time. Whenever I passed her home I would look up to her bedroom window, where she spent so much of her waking life gazing out across the high countryside to the faraway beauty of the Kentish Weald. If she was there I would wave and call out 'Hullo, Miss Bishop!' and she would wave back and give me a smile from her Madonna-like face etched so fine with the pain of many years of illness.

Anyways her young sister came over to me and took me round to her mother. I showed her what had happened and she bathed the wound with clear spring water, showered some boracic powder over it and bound it up with a long strip from a clean old sheet. Mrs Bishop said not one word to me. For she knew only too well about me and the Beale boys, with our escapades and adventures. It was retributive justice: it was not myself who was the sufferer, but my own mother to whom I would have to tell the tale of this exploit after I had gone home from the doctor's surgery stitched and bound up, and my father's pocket that would have to find the expenses for it.

So I was sent bandaged away, in the care of the young Miss Bishop, to Doctor Littledale's morning surgery at Pluckley village. This Irish doctor practised from Charing where he had his main surgery and consulting rooms in his lovely home at the top of Charing High Street, just above the Duke's Head hotel. It was not until the doctor had dressed the wound and smoothed out the rolled-up skin and flesh, and had started upon the first of the eighteen stitches he had to put in, that I began to experience real pain. There was no anaesthetic and I had to just take it! Yet, between the fascination of watching his fish-hook-like needle and the dread of being stung by a wasp that had got into the surgery and become attracted by the wound, my attention was kept off the actual pain inflicted. 'What I need for this job, young man, is a sewing machine!' remarked the doctor, when he was halfway through his hemstitching.

It was six weeks before I got my discharge and a month later my father got the bill! Five or six years passed before he finally forgot about the expense I had incurred upon him. Evidently time heals old wounds as well as doctors' old bills! For the first week I was treated as a wounded soldier by the good cottagers at Mundy Bois, as I had to stay at home until the stitches had been taken out. After that I went hop-picking with my mother and the rest of the family over at Mr Steers' farm beyond Lark Hill at Egerton; though each Tuesday for five weeks I had to go over to Pluckley to the doctor's to have the wound checked and re-dressed.

The first week was a real good week and, as I have remarked, everyone tried to help me. Mrs George Collins, with a 'You bad boy, here's a big book to read' was the first. It was one of the yearly volumes of *Young Britain* published before 1914. Then Mrs Hart, an invalid herself now, who was to die the following year, sent me round some copies of *Red Magazine* to read and young Mrs Woodcock gave me a number of

*John Bull* weeklies she had by her, along with little fancy biscuits to fortify my inner man.

\*\*\*\*\*\*

Though Pluckley was pretty well-served with water by the Mid Kent Water Company, there were isolated places, even in the 1920s, dependent upon well- and spring-water for all domestic purposes. Prebbles Hill Farm and Prebbles Hill Cottages, as well as old Mr Bishop's place, got all their water from the Prebbles Hill spring close by the north-east entrance to the great Pevington orchard. The spring flowed out from the ragstone rock and filled a deep rocky basin below, the overflow trickling away downhill into the orchard. In and around the depression holding the water frogs and toads held sway, never being disturbed or killed as the old folks said they helped keep the rocky basin clear of weeds and insects.

The big mixed fruit orchard at Prebbles Hill, belonging to Pevington Farm, was one of those places left over from the greater days of English farming. Within its wide expanse grew cherry, apple, pear, plum and damson trees; along its western edges grew the old-fashioned medlar and quince trees. Of the several varieties of apples grown, our favourites were the Old English Russets, which grew where several large walnut trees spread their shady branches in the summertime. Each year, from cherrying-time until the late autumn frosts had sweetened the rough-coated russet apples, the Beales and myself carried out a form of fruit-raiding guerrilla warfare in and around this delectable place.

Mr Beale had, on the furthermost western limit of his farm, two old cherry trees which he more or less gave over to us boys. In the evenings, when the cherries were ripening, we would sit up in their branches picking and eating the fruit. Now and again the policeman from Egerton would ride by on his bicycle and give us very suspicious looks, and we would have to him and call out 'Good evening, Police-Constable Smith'. Such friendliness from us only seemed to make him even more certain we were 'up to something'. Anyway, after he had seen Mr Beale and the situation had been explained to him, he would, when passing, give us a more or less friendly grunt to our 'Good evenings'!

******

In the deep, small valley formed by the Pevington and Elvey Lane hills ran a fast stream known as the Pevington Stream. Here it ran through Greenhill Farm land until it crossed that of Elvey Farm where it became Buss's Stream. Passing through the western lands of Elvey it went under the lane of that name to widen and deepen as it moved through the farmland of Mr Small of Pinnock Farm. It was here appropriately known as Small's Stream, until it left his land under the Pinnock Bridge from which it became the Pinnock Stream. Some miles to the south-west this fine old stream of so many names lost itself in the River Beult.

In the deep, small valley already alluded to through which ran the Pevington Stream grew a large oak tree, known to us as the Swinging Oak. Not because anyone had ever been hanged from it, but on account of us using one of the long, lower boughs as a swing in itself. Near to this tree, abutting on the stream was a low-walled and very noisome sheep-dipping tank, in which twice a year were immersed Farmer Strang's large flock of sheep, to cleanse and disinfect them from injurious insects and their grubs and eggs which like nothing better than to burrow deep into the skins of sheep and use them as full board and lodging establishments.

It was in between these sheep-dipping times, when the mood assailed us, that John, Bob and myself would go down into the valley and with large rocks gathered from the bed of the stream would hurl them into the inky water of the tank. We pretended they were huge shells and that somewhere in the tank was an enemy submarine! In would go the rocks, sending up great spouts of filthy black water, impregnated with disinfectants and chemicals. With loud cries of delight we would watch the disturbed water rocket upwards, then we would rush away from the tank to avoid the odoriferous liquid as it descended like black rain all around the walls of the sheep-dip. Close by this spot where the stream ran over gravel and between small rocks we would poke the bed of the stream to disturb the thousands of silvery-looking freshwater shrimps that abounded at this particular spot.

Many a time had Farmer Strang disturbed us while going the rounds of his lands, swinging in his oak tree; throwing rocks into his sheep-dipping tank and paddling amongst the shrimps in his silvery stream. Each time, with a bellow of wrath he would descend upon us, and we would instinctively race away up the rush-covered hillside like hares, knowing that he could never make that steep climb as could we. There he would stand, down in the valley, south of the stream, and shake his fist at us, and we would call down from our point of safety 'Old Farmer Strang, catch us if you can!'

Yet this Scottish farmer was also long to wrath, and seemed to believe in letting the sun go down upon it. He had the finest and the fastest light-van horse around our country and this fine and mettlesome animal had brought home his master times out of number, mixed up with the empty milk-churns when the farmer, too long at the flowing-bowl, had been incapable of sitting on the seat of the van, let alone able to drive. All the way from just beyond the Dering Arms down by Pluckley Station, late at night, this horse had galloped the two-and-a-half miles to Greenhill Farm to deliver itself up, with the van, the churns and the farmer. What made this fine animal so fast, so mettlesome and so intelligent was, according to its owner, the 'wee drap o' whusky' he would tip into its drinking water and the fine Gold Flake cigarettes he fed it each day! This was no leg-pull on his part, for we had seen him give the horse a 'snifter' of the whisky and feed it five cigarettes crushed up in his hand.

Society, even rural society, is made up of many types. Farmer Strang was one type in his particular way; Captain Pinkney (late of the Royal Flying Corps) was just the opposite. The captain lived at Appleby Grange at the top of the old Mundy Bois road, and he had made a prosperous scientific poultry farm upon his lands. He was abstemious to a point, and a gentleman of impeccable manners. After I left school, in August 1922, and up till March 1924, a period of roughly eighteen months, I did odd-job work for farmers and people around Mundy Bois, until I was able to get a regular situation as a learner-worker at the scientific poultry farm belonging to the Biggs Brothers at 'Roundwood' upon the high North Downs above Charing.

One of my odd jobs was digging and weeding the flower garden at Appleby Grange for Captain Pinkney's wife, quiet of voice and personality and of the most polished manners. The Pinkneys had one child, a daughter, named Isabel, a jolly and pretty little girl of, I think at that time, seven years of age. She would come out into the garden and chatter away to me. As far as I could gather, young Isabel and the Stisted children whose father Major Stisted lived at Egerton House in the next parish, over which he was the squire, schooled together under a private tutor at Egerton House. Anyway, Isabel called it her school. Once when I was busy weeding in the flowerbeds and she was busy chatting away, I asked her how she was getting along with history and geography. Nonplussed, she stared at me and courteously enquired what they were. It was my turn then to be nonplussed! So I explained that history was all about kings and queens, and battles and things of great importance that had happened since the Romans had captured Britain; and that geography was all about the world, the seas, foreign lands and their peoples, and products. She considered this for quite a minute, then said: 'Oh! I do not go to one of those sort of schools. We learn painting, embroidery, elocution and manners at our school!' That had me beaten and gave me a deep respect for such a young lady as Isabel who could learn such things as embroidery, elocution and manners.

During 1923 I was taking in the bi-weekly issue of Arthur Mee's famous *Children's Encyclopedia*, and in one number on page 2373, in the Gallery of Art section dealing with 'English Paintings of Today', I was very surprised to see the figure of Miss Isabel. No! My eyes had not deceived me; for there she was as large as life, seated on a fur-covered divan: ISABEL PINKNEY, stated the caption, BY SPENCER WATSON A.R.A. How Spencer Watson ever kept her still long enough to have been able to paint her portrait is, to me, the Eighth Wonder of the World!

*God who created me*
*Nimble and light of limb*
*In three elements free,*
*To run, to ride, to swim:*
*Not when the sense is dim,*
*But now from the heart of joy,*
*I would remember him:*
*Take the thanks of a boy.*

*Prayers*, by Canon H.C. Beeching

# CHAPTER THIRTEEN

Stoats' Island was not really such, though a fast, deep stream flowed between deep banks around the full crescent of the front of it. A waste water ditch, that divided at the rear of the 'island', gave it at flood times that appearance. The water that wound around the front was part of the Prebbles Hill stream. This island was such a secret place to me that it was never used as a strong-point or 'fort' in the chain of defences mentioned in an earlier chapter, though it was a useful spot in which to hide and the Beales and myself would meet there at times in the centre of the thicket which covered it. There we had a stone fireplace and several big rocks we used as seats. This 'island' got its name from the colony of stoats that lived in it for several years, the whole place being riddled with their burrows. They arrived there, it seemed, all of a sudden: a few pairs which were bred and bred until the place became overrun with these fierce and sinuous little killers. It was good rabbit country hereabouts, and gradually, as time went on, we noticed the rabbit population in and around Mundy Bois Wood, the Rushy Field and Home Dairy Meadow was diminishing. The stoats arrived in the winter of 1921 and stayed until the autumn of 1923 when, as suddenly as they had arrived, they disappeared. Evidently in their nearly two years' stay they had killed off the rabbits, and then, when a dearth of these animals was brought about by their continual killings, they 'shut up shop' and left the island named after them for more fruitful fields.

It was in the autumn of 1922 when I first encountered a stoat killing its prey, a rabbit. I was gathering wood-nuts from the tall hedge along the stream when I heard the piteous cries of the rabbit. Following the sounds I located it on a narrow strip of earth, a tiny 'shore' where the swift stream cut round the lower portion of Stoats' Island. Upon its back was a stoat biting away at the base of the animal's skull, far too intent to notice me. I struck the stoat a smart blow across its back with the crooked nutting-stick I carried with me. It was so surprised that it leaped into the air, turned three or four quick somersaults, dropped to the ground and tried to run in about six directions all at the same time. Then it jumped and splashed its way across the stream to disappear into the interior of the 'island'. The bewildered rabbit still crouched below, with a large bright red bead of blood oozing from the back of its neck. Suddenly, without warning, it turned left and disappeared from my sight. Climbing down the narrow strip of earth I saw in the bank the entrance to a rabbit's burrow. Down this the wounded animal had gone. Finding a large stone I jammed it hard home into the mouth of the burrow, and left for Pluckley, having in my mind the idea that on my way home in the dusk of evening I would go back there, remove the stone, and get the rabbit to add to the morrow's dinner. I did go back, but the rabbit had in my absence got over its fright and evidently its wound, raked out the earth from one side of the large stone and made good its escape. All around this area grew the trees and bushes of the wild wood-nut, and in the springtime the pale blue-flowered Lady's Smocks grew in profusion, revelling in the damp earth and the shady sides of the stream. Here too, grew all around the year various ferns, which festooned in their full seasons the earthy-smelling banks.

The northern end of Mundy Bois Wood, as it is known in the survey maps, is right opposite to Stoats' Island. It was in the early summer of 1920 that I first explored this wood, not knowing it had a name on the map. Anyway, this wooded section of Mundy Bois (actually part of the parish of Little Chart, beyond Pluckley) turned out to be such an enthralling place that after I had wandered through it and tasted its many natural pleasures in that now so far away summer's day, I called it Wonder Wood, for it was really, to my adventurous and boyish mind, a singularly wonderful place. It was the first Saturday in Whitsun in that year of 1920. The sun had been shining early and I set off down the old Mundy Bois road, past Brown's Kitchen House and onto the cart road or track leading to Horse Daisy Meadow where the pathway led up and over the heights to Prebbles Hill and Pluckley. My destination was the Beales' farm, but this particular summer's morning I did not reach it, for the sight of a moorhen slipping through a gap at the base of an impenetrable-looking hedge, where the road began at the end of the cart road, took my interest. Why was a moorhen, a water-living bird, nipping into the wood where, I was fully sure, no pond existed? The hedge, high, deep and covered with brambles, was an impassable barrier. Yet in the midst of this hedge I could discern some old wattle-gates, so often used for sheep-pens and folds. What were they doing there, like a fence? They must have been set there many years before and the blackthorn and the matthorn had sprung up and grown and grown, fully enveloping them and making a finer barrier than ever the wattle-gate fence had been! Anyway, I ferreted around and found a portion of the hedge where it was possible, after a great deal of scrambling and delving, to get over the wattle-fence and then with more pushing and thrusting to get into the wood where the moorhen had disappeared. Once on the other side I found myself standing ankle-deep in cosy mud on the margins of a small pond, almost devoid of water. A mixture of land and aquatic plants grew in profusion around its edges, and old branches from nearby trees lay criss-crossed and rotting in the pond. All around were tracks of moorhens in the mud; but all I found of their habitations were three very old rush nests at least two years old. This pond was too vulnerable against the attacks of weasels, stoats, stray cats and snakes, and doubtless the nesting moorhens had discovered this to their dismay and had abandoned it except as an occasional feeding-ground.

Leading from the pond, and appearing to run right through the lower portion of the wood, was a depression which at first sight seemed to be the bed of a dried-up stream. Yet this was not so, for on one side, along a portion of its length, I discovered what were no doubt kerbstones of Kentish Rag. Had these stones formed the edge of a path above this long depression which was evidently an ancient road continuing from where the old cart track seemed to end where the wood began? And if so, what actual purpose had the path and the sunken road filled? For at the farthest end of the wood it petered out, and there did not appear to be any continuation across the high fields to Pevington in the direction of which it pointed. Hundreds of years before Pevington, or Pivington, had been a tiny village or like community, with a church and a graveyard, and had been known as Pevington-cum-Pluckley. I worked my way along this sunken track, studded with trees and bushes and festooned with creepers which gave to the adventure a touch of the Brazilian jungle. The warm sun-laden air was alive with the hummings, whirring and movements of countless insects, while all around rabbits scuttled away and grass snakes and the grey slow-worm slithered off amidst the carpet of old leaves. This was a paradise for blackbirds and thrushes and every few yards I espied their nests in the thorny bushes. Here too, I observed thousands of strong primrose-stocks which must have made a brave display of pale gold, with their numerous blossoms, in the springtime just past.

It was just beyond this end of the sunken road that I made a most exciting discovery. Just beyond its northern bank I found an old shack beneath an oak tree. It was built of nut-wood stakes for main supports and thatched in all four sides, as well as the roof, with the thin twiggy tops of the wild wood-nut bushes. The entrance was doorless. Inside the earth floor was covered thick with rotten straw and three short round logs, standing on end, served as chairs, around a table made from another short log with a deal board nailed upon it. A couple of mildewed sacks lay in the corner with a *Daily Mail* so worn by dampness that the print was almost assuaged away, and only a few clues remained to tell me that it was this newspaper. There is no doubt that this wonderful habitation had been made by woodcutters some years before, as a shelter in wet weather, and a place where they could partake of their frugal meals. This shack later became one of our fortified links and by keeping it thatched up it proved a naturally camouflaged hiding-place; a shelter from sudden storms and a quiet spot in which to enjoy a surreptitious smoke of Park Drive, our favourite cigarettes!

The beauty and the wonder of this wood on that fine summer's day cannot be properly set down in writing: the sun-drenched adventure of it can only be recalled from memory in the mind's eye, the good Creator's greatest gift to all, the natural cinema of the mind wherein the vaults of which are stored the 'film' of everything, so that memory can always bring them out and project them in review to recall the past. Where I found the old shack the wood went steeply uphill, and here, beneath the oak trees, the wild rabbits held sway in such numbers that their burrows formed a warren. All along the sunny southern border of Wonder Wood lived the solitary wild honey bees. These insects worked burrows in the ground where the grass was short and made little rooms at their ends. In these I found their nests or honeycombs and very lovely was the taste of this wildest of wild honey! Here I came upon the Lightning Oak, a tree struck from top to toe by such a heavenly flash of electricity. Yet it had not harmed this great tree enough to stay its growth. In later years in summer, I would sit beneath its shade and read the books of Captain Brereton, and

Herbert Strang, and in between chapters would pause to listen to the leaves rustling above me, and watch their shadows dappling the ground beneath. I would near the corncrake call and the chirruping of the baby partridges out in Horse Daisy Meadow; watch the mother rabbits lie to give suck to their little ones; hear the grasshopper fiddling and follow the slow erratic flying of the big brimstone butterflies.

******

The exploration of Small's Stream in the summer of 1921, the year of the Great Drought, was one of our biggest exploring adventures. As I had explained in an earlier chapter this stream came down from Pevington passing through the farmlands of Farmers Strang, Buss and Small. In the torrid month of July 1921, John, Bob and myself took upon ourselves the task of tracing the stream from the Pevington area right across to far-off Pluckley Pinnock. Needless to relate the stream had dried up, for even the springs had ceased to flow. Anyway, on a blazing July afternoon we descended Rushy Field and at the ford near Farmer Strang's sheep-dipping tank we set off to follow the course of the stream. Rounding it by Stoats' Island we continued on to where a wide bridge composed of old railway sleepers crossed it before it met the stream made by the water bubbling up between the rocks at the end of the old cart road. This spring had stopped rising and the stream was empty of water. Where these two streams met in the north-east corner of Horse Daisy Meadow they formed into one and flowed into a large field which adjoined Plateau Field. From there we followed it until it twisted and turned to debauch into a large pond named Deep Pond in Pinnock Bridge Meadow. Here we found old Pecker Brunger busy digging out the dried-up pond. He was cutting out the silted-up bed of the pond to a depth of another four feet, so that when the rains came – we thought they would never come again – and the stream flowed once more, the pond would have a depth in the middle of quite eight feet. Pecker was cutting the drying mud out with a long-handled wooden spade, about fifteen inches long, six inches at its top and tapering to around four inches. The surface of it was slightly concave. To stop the mud from sticking to this wooden shovel – which he called a 'pond-digger' – Pecker kept dipping it in a pail of water to keep its surfaces moist and clean. The parcels of mud he kept throwing up and over the banks of the pond resembled, in a way, the peat turves as they are cut in the bogs in Ireland; and when they dried out in the sun looked even more like that. Old Pecker showed us some 'fossil' moorhen's eggs he had dug out which he reckoned might be years old, and several clean skeletons of field-mice, and rabbits that had drowned in the pond. Some of these had met their deaths, so he reckoned from the depths he had disinterred them, twenty or more years before!

Such ponds as Deep Pond, however deep they may be, gradually silt up over the years, especially if the streams feeding them are deep and fast and flow alongside cultivated land whose water-channels drain into them. We continued to follow the stream and came to where it passed under a brick-built pinnock bridge from which the field came by its name. On either side of this bridge the stream ran between banks of some steepness, and near the bridge grew in profusion those peculiar aquatic plants called water-figwort. Near this bridge, and now embedded in the weed, we saw the great smooth rock, weighing about a hundredweight, upon which I had tested my young wiry strength the previous summer by pushing and tugging at it to topple it off the edge of the bridge into the sparkling stream. Here we had found that past summer a couple of red-clay darin pipes sticking out of the muddy bank. These so mystified us that we thought they might be Roman remains. We asked Mr Jesse Buss at Elvey Farm about them and he assured us that they were not old Roman relics but some field drainage pipes set there back in Queen Victoria's days. The stream went on and passed out into Three Oaks Meadow, but we had to make a detour on account of the hedge-junction through which it passed as just at that point the branches criss-crossed and the vegetation combining with the tough rushes made an almost impenetrable barrier, particularly owing to the steep banks. So we went on all fours under a wide break through the maythorn hedge further over. Beneath this break in normal rain-weather there would be a wide shallow pool. In the early summer, when the scented white may blossomed, the petals would fall to drop upon the scintillating surface of this pool, making it look fairy-like and of an exciting ethereal loveliness.

Once in Three Oaks Meadow we picked up the stream once more. Here it ran, when not dried out as it was this year, between deep banks overhung with rushes and long grasses and all kinds of flowering plants as well as with streamers of the wild brambles. One could not see the water flowing, but it could be heard beneath the riot of vegetation as it rushed and gurgled, sending out whispering and tinkling sounds like soft music. Following the course of the stream bed we came to Owl Pond which took its overflow in heavy rain-weather and where, just past it, it swung sharply right to flow downhill away through a deep channel cut deeper and wider after each floodwater season. Then it swept sharp left to cut straight through a widish mud-flat overgrown with grass, this mud-flat having been possibly a hundred years before an extensive pond that like so many such ponds had silted up by the earth particles deposited there by the stream year after year. Here the stream went under a wide pinnock bridge. It was here where I spent, from time to time, in the heavy rain seasons, many hours floating the empty cardboard shot-cases gathered around the fields where, after the 'guns' had fired their single- or double-barrelled shotguns at partridges and rabbits, they were ejected from the breeches and left to lie in the grass. These shot-cases or cartridges I would drop, usually three at a time, into the rushing, boiling stream, where they would twirl and bob in the waters to disappear under the bridge, to be swiftly snatched out of the stream as they swept out from under the pinnock. In my boyish imagination these were swimmers who had been swept over Niagara Falls and who were braving the rapids below them, fighting for their lives in the terribly swift and treacherous currents beneath the falls.

Not far from this pinnock the stream, now several feet wide, disappeared under Elvey Lane. Under this bridge we went, crawling on hands and knees over the rock-strewn bed, splashing through muddy pools still existing under the shade of the bridge overhead. The air here was damp and cool and quite a joy to us after the weeks of scorching sunshine we had been experiencing. It took us some time to negotiate this part of our exploration, but at last we emerged, splashed with mud, covered with cobwebs and with knees and hands scratched in a score of places. Along the wide bed of this watercourse we travelled as through a tunnel, with the trees and bushes on either side forming an archway overhead through which the sun's rays could hardly penetrate. Rabbits scuttled ahead of us, as well as many field-mice, a few water-rats and, slithering with soft nestling sounds, grass snakes moved swiftly to escape us strange beings who had suddenly invaded their previously unchallenged realm. We were still on Farmer Buss's property, so here the stream was named after this gentleman, yet we had always called in Small's Stream from Pluckley Pinnock, where it passed from Farmer Small's fields right back to the Elvey Lane road bridge which abutted on either sides of the lane to Farmer Buss's most southernly property. At last we emerged into a wide space, lit up by the sunshine pouring through a break in the trees and hedge. This opening had been there beyond memory and had evidently been cut as an opening for cows to come down from the large meadow opposite to drink water at the stream which, at this point, ran shallow over a rather gravelly bottom, which I had come to name Gravel Shallows. In normal times, when the stream was running, we would come to paddle, revelling in the coldness of the water as it played around our ankles to send long tinglings up our spines to cool our sun-warmed heads.

At Gravel Shallows we left the stream, for the bed continued on through the tunnel made by the high banks and the trees and hedges on either side. Soon we came out onto the lands of Farmer Small of Pinnock Farm to continue our exploration of the stream. Mr Small was a man greatly interested in the conservation of water for his cows and sheep during the drier months of the year, and he had made a dam where the stream flowed out from the 'tunnel' against the depletion of water by a continued spell of dry weather. This dam served his sheep for drinking purposes and kept them from getting into the deep stream for their drinking water. For it so often happened that one or more were drowned every year by getting into deep ditches and streams after water and so drowning or getting stuck in the mud, their barrel-like bodies being so awkward to turn back into the upright position. The dam, that year of 1921, was also dried out, and wide, deep fissures split the hard mud all over, looking like forked lightning tying itself in knots. In previous summers we had enjoyed paddling here and had tried our hand at 'log-rolling' like the timber-jacks in faraway Canada, with a round log about nine inches in diameter. Our efforts usually ended with being precipitated into the waters of the dam with a loud splash. The wall of this dam was built up of three-inch-deep planks about nine inches wide. These the farmer had placed above each other, the ends being driven deep into the soft muddy banks. Stout posts front and back of these planks kept the dam wall in position, the posts being held against the heavy planks by four-inch nails. When the planks expanded with the soaking from the water they closed up tight to form a solid surface, backing the water and so forming quite a small pond.

From here we journeyed on, following the dry stream bed as it wound along towards Pluckley Pinnock in the warm hazy distance. On our left, to the north, Farmer Small's large section of grassland, part of the great Pluckley Ley, stretched away with the dancing heat waves, the earth bone-hard and deeply fissured, the grass shrivelled and brown. On the other side of the stream was the farmer's long, narrow ley-field bordering the road from the pinnock to the crossroads at Mundy Bois. Owing to the dreadfully hot summer and the many weeks of absent rain, this long cultivated field laid out for crop rotation was a sight we had never before held. The corn and the oats grew sparse, pale-yellow, thin and brittle-looking. The field had been burnt to a deep black and the peas shrunken tangles of sickly grey bines. The young mangold-wurzel plants had ceased to struggle in their fight for existence and a crop of lucerne and clover showed only dully green patches where in normal times there would have been a luscious spread of tall green grasses with a thick base of sweetly-scented red clover.

Eventually we arrived at our journey's end, the Pluckley Pinnock, where the bridge carried the road over this part of Small's Stream. Here everything was dried right out, even the bed of the stream under the bridge. We went under it and discovered in the mud, still slightly soft, many freshwater mussels of a large size. Finding these freshwater shellfish suddenly recalled to memory that I had read a story in a comic at some time about the pearls that these molluscs contain; for these mussels of our inland rivers and streams are the freshwater equivalent of the pearl-bearing oysters of the sea. So John, Bob and I gathered as many as we could find and, taking them to the side of the road by the bridge, we opened them with our shet-knives, the dialect for the common pen-knife or 'shut-knife'. But these mussels had never tried to emulate their cousins of the deep seas and our vision of sudden wealth from a pile of large freshwater mussel pearls faded away into the scorching air.

Just by the old bridge was an oak tree, with a sparse circlet of small branches around its top, for the upper part had been blown or struck off beyond the limits of memory and the tree had become fully hollow right down to ground level. Just inside the top, a pair of pied wagtails built their nests and raised their families for three years running. There was a legend about this oak that my grandfather, Jesse Pile, had told me. It was stated that once a highwayman had hidden from the Bow Street Runners in this hollow tree, hoping to escape detection, but the high-tobyman's horse would not move away from the tree and the Runners discovered his whereabouts. As he would not come out, and as he could have easily shot dead with his pistols any one of them foolhardy enough to climb up to the opening at the top of the oak, the Bow Street men sought out and found a split in the tree and, thrusting a sword through it, skewered the highwayman inside, and so killing him. One day, on my way home from school I was tempted to emulate the highwayman's supposed feat and climbed down inside this tree. When I had grubbed around inside and poked the earth to see if any golden guineas might still be hidden there, supposing that the 'Stand-and-deliver!' gentleman had had any and perhaps had dropped some, I found to my dismay that I could not get out! There was not a great deal of traffic along the road just outside the hollow oak, and the evening was pulling in fast for it was late autumn. Anyway, I found at length, at arm's stretch above my head, a split in the side of the oak. Into this I put my first finger of my right hand and by sheer tenacity hauled myself up to where my left hand could catch hold upon a hardened protuberance. When I came to disengage my finger I discovered that it had become tightly jammed. By much wriggling and upward pulling it became free, leaving a fair amount of skin behind. Eventually I climbed out and got back safe to earth – outside. If I had slipped when my almost whole weight depended upon one thin finger, I should have been precipitated downwards, and quite possibly have had the finger torn out from its lower joint! Yet I saw no fear in those days.

Within the memory of my Grandmother Pile, an old lady who sold watercress to the people of the nearby villages caught herself afire by the bridge at this pinnock and was burnt to death. Evidently she had been busy gathering watercress from the Small's Stream, to replenish her basket, and afterwards had sat down by the roadside to enjoy a quiet smoke of her old clay pipe. She had nodded off to sleep that day of late summer and her pipe must have fallen into her lap and set light to her clothing. Then there grew up a ghost legend about this spot where the old watercress woman had so tragically died: on the anniversary of her sad and shocking end it was said that her ghost appeared wrapped in flames, and screaming for help! Not only was the stream here noted for its watercress, but also for its eels. Across the other side of the road a sullage or waste-water ditch ran into the stream where it began its run through the farmland of Farmer Heathfield. This odoriferous spot I named Smelly Ditch. It evidently drained the sewage from cess-pits of the cottages, and the big red brick villa of Mr Evenden on Pinnock Hill about a hundred yards away. Yet here at the Smelly Ditch the first wild-nut catkins appeared year after year; and around the area of the tall white signpost near the edge of this ditch grew the tallest and most luxuriant stinging-nettles I ever saw.

Perhaps the tall signpost at the Pluckley Pinnock, at that time, was the most heavily-endowed of all such indication of places and distances. It had four fingers. One pointed to PLUCKLEY STATION and ASHFORD; one to PLUCKLEY THORNE, PLUCKLEY, LITTLE CHART and CHARING;

another to SMARDEN BELL and HEADCORN, and the other to MUNDY BOIS, EGERTON, ULCOMBE and BOUGHTON MALHERBE. John, Bob and I would take it in turns to climb to the top of the post and, while it creaked and swayed rather ominously over the bed of giant nettles, would chant as a challenge to each other the 'dare' – 'I'm the King of the Castle and you're the Smelly Rascal!' Then one day Mr Evenden, prim and neat, came by carrying his inevitable small basket of fresh eggs. He had long ago made his pile of money and retired. He stopped to stare at us, and then to speak, remarking: 'It is a very great pity indeed, that your respected parents cannot find some useful tasks for young lads like you!' We gazed at him in silence – silence we had found from long-standing to be one of our greatest weapons. Wavering under our quietness and our coldly staring eyes he walked away towards his large red-brick villa on the hill, as prim and proper as ever was and with that little bit of swank he always affected in his gait. After he had got well away we called out 'Old Cocky Evenden!' and slipped away. On the following Monday morning, after prayers in the big classroom at Pluckley School, our school-gaffer Mr Turff, though he mentioned no names, gave out a lecture about young rascals with nothing better to do than climb signposts and call after a highly-respected member of the Pluckley community. Anyway, Mr Evenden had been known among the more ancient inhabitants of our village as 'Cocky' for at least three decades, and when once a nickname is given it sticks like glue!

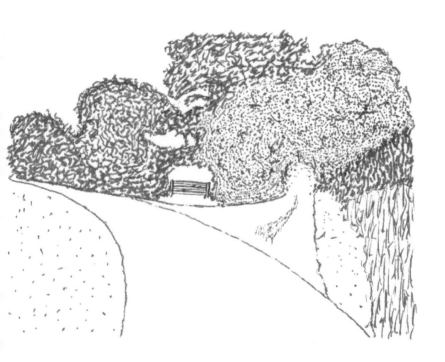

*We are born to seek what we can never find!*

*It is the greatest game of hide and seek that was ever invented. God has hidden His truth, and we shall never find it on this Earth; but He has made the search for it so exciting and splendid that, although we know we can never discover it, the greatest of the sons of men have found their highest happiness in this search. To this every age bears witness.*

'Ideas: the great words that stir the hearts of all Mankind', *The Children's Encyclopedia*, edited by Arthur Mee

# CHAPTER FOURTEEN

On the land of Farmer Small, not far from his farmhouse and the Pinnock Stream, was a large sheet of water, half-encircled with very wild growths of maythorn bushes and a few may trees. On account of the prickliness of these growths this pond was known to us as Thorny Pond. This was the largest of the ponds in the parish of Pluckley, excepting the great sheet of very deep water called the Pluckley Clayhole, near to the Brick and Tile Works close to the railway station. This later water was really a small lake and not classifiable as just a pond. In the year of the Great Drought of 1921, even Thorny Pond began to dry up and as the banks became more exposed it looked even larger than it was when full. No-one ever fished here, and as nearly all the fish-ponds had dried up I went one lovely evening to try my luck there. For a long while I fished but did not get a bit. Almost in desperation I made a last cast, not too far out. Suddenly the float bobbed under and I felt the weight of a big fish at the line. I never 'played' a fish. With a mighty heave and up-throw over my head I jerked the rod and line up and over. Our flashed a fine fish, to land on the grass behind me. It was a lovely roach, which on being weighed by Mr Goldup at his home The Hollies near the Rose and Crown, just within the boundaries of Pluckley, this excellent catch went two-and-a-quarter pounds in weight.

Of course the Goldups and the Coopers at the inn wanted to know where I had caught it. When I told them they were surprised, for they had never known a fish to be taken from Thorny Pond. 'Must have been the only fish in there' remarked Mr Goldup, the ex-police constable turned farmer. 'No doubt it was real famished through the drought and just snapped up your bait. You wouldn't have caught it otherwise' he continued.

Anyway, the next day I ran into Bert Adams, who we called 'Sloppy' on account of him being quiet, well-mannered and behaved, which was so unlike the majority of us lads. He was going fishing; so was I. I thought he was going to try his luck in Chapel Pond in the field adjoining Pluckley Chapel on the Pluckley-Smarden road. He told me he was going to fish the Thorny Pond. I asked him why, and he replied that his grandfather, old 'Squeaker' Pile, a near-relation of my own grandfather 'Independence' Pile, had told him that there used to be really big fish in the Thorny Pond, and he was going to try his luck. Then I told him of the giant roach I had landed there the previous evening and so we went off to try our luck. By the end of the morning he had landed three good roach, weighing half a pound, three quarters of a pound and a pound-and-a-half respectively. I captured two half-pounders and a three-quarter pounder. No-one had ever taken such large roach in the ponds of the village in the memory of us boys. What I had discovered had been a known fact to old Squeaker, who farmed a small place between Cooper Farm and Chambers Green.

******

Opposite to Mr Small's Pinnock Farm was the tiny farm of old Farmer Stamford. Whether Old Stamford's place had a name we never knew, but Bob Beale and I always called it Broken Legs Farm, on account of Mr Stamford having such long and crooked legs. He told us once that, owing to having been kicked by various horses and from awkward falls, he had broken one leg three times and the other four! Sometimes Bob and I would go home together 'my way' round by the road. We would get into this old farmer's cart-lodge and climb under the dim roof.

Two of the roof boards were broken at one end and we would call out, if we saw him pottering around his house or his yard, 'Old Farmer Stamford!' At once he lost his temper and would look angrily around to see the culprits. Of course he could not, for after calling out we immediately withdrew our heads. This game would go on until we grew tired of it when we would slip away and run softly away along the grass verge of the road to the Pinnock. The old farmer would search high and low, muttering to himself and calling out 'Show yourselves, ye varmints, for I can see ye!' all this time waving his knotting walking-stick and whacking it about him. He never found us and became more mystified every occurrence, until at last he gave up trying and so, as far as Bob and I were concerned, the fun of our little 'calling-him-over' game lost its spice and we gave up tormenting the crooked-legged old gentleman.

Pinnock Farm was the only real old-fashioned one in the parish of Pluckley. Here lived Mr Small, a likeable and gentlemanly man, and his wife, one of the dearest and most motherly souls in the parish. With them lived their servant, who had been with them ever since she had left school, sharp-speaking, plump and short Jane Pile, whose sister Mary Jane Pile was servant and milkmaid for another Mr Small over at a farm just below Pluckley Thorne on the road to the Chapel. This was another farm we did not know by name so we always referred to it as 'Mary Jane's Farm', and very appropriate it turned out to be in later years, for Mary Jane eventually married her former master whose wife had died many, many years before.

Pinnock Farm would boast of its own home-cured bacon and gammon hocks; cream, butter and cheese also. Mrs Small and Jane Pile baked their own bread, cakes and buns. They had their own fresh-killed pork, veal and poultry. They pickled eggs and salted pork. The only thing they did not make was beer, though in years gone by even this had been brewed there. This was a really self-contained farm, depending hardly at all upon the tradesmen of the village. Farmer Small also possessed the finest and the fiercest sheepdog in the parish. At least a dozen lean cats, of all shades and markings, roamed the farm buildings and the rick-yard. These were the ratters and the mousers who kept the farm clear of these destructive pests. After dinner, our Jane would bring out a large platter of mixed vegetables and bread, warmed up, and give them to the cats. She would knock upon the dish with a great spoon and the mousers would rush in from all points of the compass to be fed. One day I asked Jane Pile why she never gave them any meat. 'Meat, my boy,' she replied, 'ain't good for working cats. It makes them sleepy and lazy. They have to hunt and find their own meat, which is ratsies and mousies! And they only get this one meal a day, so's they ain't overfed.' Brilliant reasoning, I thought, and tucked the fact away in case I ever became a farmer and had twelve cats like Farmer Small had.

To the left of Pinnock Farm, and behind some small outbuildings, lay a rectangular pond built in on three sides with bricks and rocks. The field end was open for cattle to come to drink. On the roadside section of this pond, which abutted on the back garden of Pinnock Cottage, in which lived another Small, a nephew, or so we believed him to be of Farmer Small, the pond was flanked with trees which overhung it to about halfway out and the roots of which had worked their way into it.

So, for quite halfway out, down the whole side of this piece of water, under the water the rocks held sway, entangling the old branches as they fell, year by year, from the trees into the water. This formed an underwater matrix, amidst which lived and swam hundreds of nice little roach. Yet they never left this entangled part and we could not fish for them, for every cast would have meant a snared line and the loss of innumerable floats, hooks and lines. Yet the other half of the pond housed thousands of sticklebacks and minnows, and these never crossed over into roach territory. It seemed as if a line of demarcation had been put right down the centre by Nature. This pond was clear as crystal and we could watch the fish swimming about, not just in twos or threes, but in whole battalions! Here in the palmy days of summer we would fish for the voracious sticklebacks and minnows with largish worms stuck on bent pins attached to string lines. We could see the small fish come up to nibble them and then quickly gulp them down gollop-by-gollop. Before they had time to disgorge we pulled them out and pulled the works out of their still-working jaws and popped them into jam jars.

When we tired of this sport we would count up our catches and then return them back home to the pond. Sometimes we caught as many as two hundred or more in two or three hours. Not collectively, but individually! And while we fished, 'Jammy' Small would keep an eye on us from Pinnock Cottage. He got this nickname from Bob, for this Small earned his living by making all kinds of delicious jams, preserves and pickles. We would call out to him as he went about his business around the village: 'How's the jam today, Mr Jammy?' And he would smile back and simper: 'None the better for your asking – you saucy boys!' This would send us into whoops of joy and uncontrollable mirth.

On the land of Farmer Small was another pond, we had named Round Pond, on account of it being really circular. It had a few maythorn bushes around part of its rim and owing to the always muddy-looking state of the water we did not know that, hidden beneath its surface, were many tough roots from the bushes on its bank. In this pond existed a few very small roach wary of being caught. One afternoon I had cast my hook and line further out, and shortly afterwards, the float bobbed down. With my usual do-or-die fishing method I up-handed mightily and the tension in my line nearly pulled me forward into the pond. Again I struck, this time with all my might! The line snapped and I was catapulted backwards flat upon my back, the cloud-flecked summer sky above me. 'What a whopping fish!' I thought. Then I got up and looked out across the water. The flat still stood upright in the pond. Mystified that the giant fish had not taken it down with it, I went round to investigate and then found that all I had really caught was one of the larger underwater roots of the maythorn bush!

It was here that the Luckhurst boys, who lived at this time in one of the small cottages at Pluckley Thorne, known as Thorne Cottages, told me about a mysterious blue bird they had seen at the Round Pond and one of them, my old schoolchum 'Punch' Luckhurst, described it to be so swift in flight that it was just 'a flash of blue'. After many waits in the vicinity of the pond I finally discovered what kind it was: it was a kingfisher and it nested at the end of a tunnel in the clay bank. This was the only kingfisher ever seen in the village, and later I was able to trace its movements, though it must have had a mate, as it spent its time between a pond in Thorne Ruffits, a pond in Ammet Meadow, and the small Round Pond. This formed a triangle of flight, the pond in Ammet Meadow forming the apex.

******

Thorne Ruffits, which lay below the Pluckley Thorne (a hamlet) was really a rough or 'ruffit' stretch of woodland. In the centre of this long and narrow wood was a pond, also long and narrow, to which I gave the name of Swampy Pond. This wood was a mass of underbrush tangled with briars; a difficult place to explore. I well remember one lovely morning in June, it being a Saturday, I set off from Munday Bois to try and penetrate 'The Ruffits' as my grandfather always called them. After much dodging and crawling I reached the centre of the wood and found the pond. And what a pond! Stretching out of sight on either side its extreme ends became covered in by the underbush. It was pretty wide, but not more than six inches deep in the middle and was filled with all kinds of aquatic plants, and the dead leaves of many an autumn past. Around its tree-lined margins grew tufts of rushes and in these rushes were many nests of moorhens.

Moorhens were scampering away all around me, and when I had gone all round this swampy piece of water I had found no less than thirty-six nests of these birds, from those just being built to others completed and with one or more brown splotched eggs. In all I counted sixty-one eggs! Here indeed was a super colony of moorhens never matched anywhere else in the whole of the surrounding parishes – not even at the big Pluckley Clayhole where some two dozen pairs of moorhens were usually to be found. What visions of bubbling billy-cans filled with eggs boiling, over crackling camp-fires of old try twigs, swam into my mind's eye! Yet apart from this wonderful gastronomic material was that comprising the ethereal. For all around the ground was covered with a carpet of bluebells which drenched the humid air with their marvellous perfume, and growing among them were the tall pink spikes of early spring orchids to add to the colourful bounty of it all!

Outside of this tangled yet glorious place, at one end, lay a deep, roundish pond, known at the Thorne Pond, used as a drinking-place for sheep and cows roaming the great stretch of flat grassland called The Ley. A deep-banked stream ran into this pond and from it, to the pinnock-bridge some fifty yards away grew the most luscious watercress. This stream was known as Watercress Stream, as it had been named by my great-grandfather Pile, who had lived with his family at Pluckley Thorne in the long ago. It was from this place that I rescued a full-grown lamb from drowning one day on my way home from school. After a great deal of struggling, pulling and pushing, I eventually got the lamb up and over the high ditch and safely out to the short grass of the old ley, where its mother awaited it. Never was there such a muddied pair as this lamb and I! And how surprising was its weight, though it did not seem all that big. Anyway I plodded off home in the gathering dusk, covered, I presumed, with glory, and most certainly with mud!

******

Pluckley Ley, or the Old Ley, was the greatest piece of finest grazing-land outside of Romney Marsh. When the Great War of 1914-18 was in progress this wonderfully flat-surfaced ley became an aerodrome to bring thoughts of that terrible conflict nearer home, and with its fighter planes and airmen a new phase of mechanical and social life into the village. The war ended, it reverted to pasture again, and where the wartime biplanes had flown in and out over it herds of sheep came to graze. Even down to 1922, some four years after the Great War had passed into world history, in the Thorne Ruffits piles of rusting tins that had once held 'Gargoyle' Mobiloil could still be found, and hundreds of empty salmon, bully beef and 'plum and apple' tins unexpectedly encountered; legacies of the Boys in Blue who had once flown high in the bright blue sky.

During the early years of the Peace this ley, which had now become more popularly known to all as the Landing Ground, still retained an interest for the Royal Air Force and civilian airlines. When the RAF was on night manoeuvres, sometimes extending over quite some time, these great flares were put out on the ley, in position to form a huge letter 'L'. Dusty Buss, the Pluckley miller's son, used to be given the job of tending to them, and he had to be up and about all night. With some straw-jacketed wattle gates he would make a kind of small fold and cover this over with a canvas tarpaulin. Inside this he would sit if things were quiet and shelter if the weather was bad. Bob, John and myself would keep him company for a couple of hours most evenings and help him inspect the flares and watch and listen for aircraft.

This old landing ground was a real boon to civilian air pilots in difficulties. Once, in 1921, a two-seater biplane with two French airmen made a forced descent when the right side lower wing developed a long tear, believed to have been made by a bird in flight. After a delay of several hours some doped silk was brought into the village, and the two jabbering airmen, helped by young Tom Black who was a handy lad with his hands, fitted the patch over the tear. Tom was suitably rewarded by the airmen with a five-bob tip in English money. And what a wonderful send-off they were given! For nearly all the boys in the village were there to see the repair made and the plane take off. How they shouted and yelled as the biplane taxied over the sward and took the air! All the snatches of 'French' that they had heard during the 1914-18 War formed a farewell to the *aviateurs*. These lusty cries will never grow less: '*Au revoir!*' '*Bon jour!*' '*Parley voo!*' '*Vive la France!*' '*Intent cordial!*' and many more, just as fascinating and curious! And still the planes flew over Pluckley; those of the RAF, private civilian pilots and the great thrumming passenger planes which, when making their way into the teeth of a really stiff wind seemed to be without apparent forward movement! Those were the great days when planes were kept together by struts and wires; and the RAF, and not so long before the Royal Flying Corps, was really feeling its wings and cutting its back teeth!

******

When the shooting season commenced in the autumn, Bob, John and I, if we were not employed at pheasant beating in the woods, or driving partridges in the fields, would follow any party of 'guns' we happened across on Saturdays. The idea of this tagging-along, always out of sight of the 'guns', the beaters and in particular the gamekeepers, was to pick up any stray birds that came out way that had been hit and not mortally wounded, which crawled and fluttered into the hedges and ditches. These we claimed for our own flesh-pots, as we considered Sir Henry Dering, Baronet, to have sufficient for his own table for a long time to come. Especially as much of this game was hung in the larders until it was ripe, or sweet, and as my Aunt Fanny, who worked at old Colonel Cheeseman's at Little Chart, had often told me, 'My dear boy, they keep them hanging until they are simply crawling with maggots!'

It was the early autumn of 1923 when the leaves had hardly turned to colour, and so wild had been the weather and without frost, that the leaves of the stouter oaks were as green as in the summertime gone by, that one Saturday morning we tangled with the advance guard of Sir Henry Dering's shooting party out for the day, working the Pevington-Greenhill areas where they ran close to the boundaries of Mundy Bois. We three were at the old duckpond near Rushy Meadow, playing at 'Royal Engineers building a bridge while under fire from German artillery'. This was one of our favourite pastimes as it involved mud, water, danger and adventure. There was little doubt that we were sweet and playful little souls in these now faraway days!

The main idea was for one of us to place stones in the pond at two places across its width, and then lay along two old planks we kept handy in the deep ditch at Stoats' Island nearby. While all this was going on, the 'Royal Engineers' would be subjected to a crossfire of clods of earth from the 'German gunners'. This meant that if they did not get clouted with the lumps of soil they got well and truly splashed with mucky water thrown up by the 'shell-bursts'. Bob happened to be the 'R.E.' at that time, and he had done pretty well. The rock support had been laid down, and the planks placed in position, and he was halfway across when the real enemy was sighted by John who was on the higher ground. 'Look out, Bob! Look out, Fred!' he cried. 'Here comes Sir Henry and his lot!' Bob went forward, then back, and the bridge slipped over and shot him into the pond. In less than a minute all three of us were safe, high up in a small oak tree, well hidden in the thick foliage. We peeped out between the clusters of leaves, watching the comings and goings of the party from the 'Big House' – Surrenden Mansion.

We nearly fell out of the tree with suppressed laughter on one or two occasions, for some of the 'guns' couldn't have hit an elephant at five yards' range. To these, their gun-loaders were sympathetic, the gamekeepers choleric! Sir Henry, a great man with the double-barrelled shotgun, was slamming off right, left and centre, but doing but very little damage to the birds hurtling overhead. For the pheasant had been raised up on the steep slopes of the rises forming the hills and folds of outer Greenhill, and they were flying high and fast by the time they came into range of the guns who stood about twenty yards forward of the duckpond. Then one bird that had evidently been 'winged' swooped down right at one of the guns who was a poor shot (the type we called a 'rabbit-pauncher'). Either panic-stricken or full of do-or-die spirit he blazed both barrels off at once almost in the face of the plunging pheasant. Hit it he did, yet his triumph was short-lived, for all he got for his pains was a blood-speckled skeleton. For the terrific force of the double explosion and the full number of the lead pellets had stripped the doomed game-fowl of its feathers and flesh!

\*\*\*\*\*\*

Elvey Lane, which ran from the Top Road at Prebbles Hill, past Prebbles Hill Farm, old Captain Bishop's cottage and the Prebbles Hill Cottages overlooking Pevington orchard, was a real wild and little-attended thoroughfare until it reached Elvey Farm where it was kept up as a good third class road (or lane) until it came out to meet the Pinnock-Mundy Bois road not far from the Rose and Crown inn. The banks on either side of it, above Elvey Farm until it flattened out near the big Top Field, would be decorated in the summertime with great clumps of fool's parsley, knapweed, scabious and flowering thistles. On any hot summer's afternoon it was a delight to walk down this steep, loose rock-strewn way to see the dozens of Red Admiral and peacock sporting about. Anywhere else in the parishes around you might see one or two of each in a day's march, yet here in this wild stretch of old-time lane they just swarmed in the warmth, quietness and wildness of Nature left alone to her own devices.

Elvey Farm at threshing time in the late autumn was a great place of interest to the Beales and myself. As the wheat, barley and oat stacks in the rick-yard diminished under the devouring maw of the clattering threshing-machine worked off the great traction engine, we would go around the stacks watching eagerly for the glints from the eyes of the disturbed mice within them. As the sheaves were removed and the stacks became lower, the mice would work their way to the outside of the stack, staying about six inches from the ends of the straw stalks. As soon as we saw the whites of their eyes our bare hands would plunge in and hold them captive. In this way we would catch as many as four or five hundred in a day for Farmer Buss and we always took at least a couple of dozen home with which to treat our neighbour's cats. What a grand feed they had!

Not far below Elvey Farm, down the old lane, was a pond known to us as Danger Swamp. It was more of a swamp than a pond, being full of the sharp-leaved rushes and tangled trees which grew out of its waters. It was here where several pairs of moorhens lived and nested annually – right out in the middle! Though we could not reach their nests by wading we nevertheless managed to get some of their eggs. This was done by securing a tablespoon to the end of a twelve-foot pole and dipping the eggs out, one by one. Now and again we lost one if the pole slipped, the egg falling into the root-tangled depths. Eggs taken under such circumstances always tasted better than others when cooked, no doubt in the same way as 'stolen apples being the sweetest' – even if they were green and as tart as vinegar! The other side of this pond lay Honey Farm Field and at the back of Honey Farm a meadow called, in the dialect of the district, Ammet Meadow: 'ammet' being the country name for the common ant. This meadow was alive with them, and their hills covered almost every foot of ground. On the low bank of this field going along the right-o'-way towards Pluckley Thorne grew a tiny silvery-green plant called 'Mouse's Hair'. It was here that, in the long ago, my grandmother and greater-grandmother had come to pick the leaves and taken them home to boil with black liquorice to make a wonderful cough and cold cure. This plant grew only here, not being found anywhere else in the surrounding parishes.

*The gentle flowers,*
*Retired and stooping through the wilderness,*
*Talk of humility, and peace, and love.*

*... and happy is he who has learned to listen to their voice.*

*Sacred Philosophy of the Seasons*, by the Rev. Henry Duncan DD

# CHAPTER FIFTEEN

Half a mile below Pluckley village was the hamlet of Pluckley Thorne, comprised at the time of these chronicles of a row of single-storey cottages; a row a little farther over of some substantial two-storey brick-built cottages; an old private house with a boot-repairer's shop alongside; the premises of the inn called The Blacksmith's Arms and its adjoining newspaper and grocery shop, smithy and club-room. Then not far away was Thorne House (or Farm) and by the Misses Maylam a large private house called Fir Tree Cottage. The Blacksmith's Arms had for its landlord a very busy and sporting man called James Barry Blackman who took a great interest in all sports from chess to horse-racing. Not only was he one of the village's two blacksmiths, but also added to these the titles of grocer, newsagent and postman! He did all the shoeing of the hunting-horses of the gentry round about as well as those attached to the kennels at Smarden.

Mr Wood, of Forge House, halfway up Pluckley Hill, would never let us boys go around to his smithy unless it was on business, when we required him to make for us light iron hoops for trolling along the lanes or roads. These cost sixpence each, and a special hook for the hoop was threepence extra. This hook was of thin round iron and had a curl at one end to hold the hoop up, and as one ran along, the hoop moved in this open 'loop' and so cut out the business of beating the hoop along as one had to if using the 'old-fashioned' wooden stick. Oh, yes! We were very progressive in our village!

Yet James Barry Blackman, who had several boys of his own and two daughters who were the greatest tomboys for miles around, never chased us away from his forge. Then we would watch the whole process of a horse being shod, as well as seeing him or his second son 'Flannel' knock out a shoe from the glowing iron. How we loved the sparks that flew, and the gleaming scale beaten off the red-hot iron! The hissing of the red-hot metal as it was plunged into the water to temper it and the cloud of warm steam that arose! At the back of the forge was a pond called, of course, Forge Pond. This was circular in shape and very deep. In it lived many sizeable roach as no-one was allowed to fish there. Here, very often could be seen, almost submerged, one or other of the old inn's two dartboards. They were, from time to time, tethered by a piece of cord to a stick in the bank and allowed to soak and so swell up, making the wood tighter. This method prolonged the life of such boards.

Not far from this pond was another known as Pluckley Thorne Pond, and sometimes Cottage Pond as it was on the land adjoining the two-storey cottages nearby. This was a deep and oval piece of water, full of minnows – thousands of them – and frogs – hundreds of 'em! The noise made by the croakings of the frogs was often very annoying, and the cottagers now and again would have a frog hunt and kill as many as a hundred or more at a time. One old veteran we caught alive had only three legs, having lost one either in battle or in one of the hunts. Ernest Blackman, whom we called 'Nibbo' because he was the blacksmith's youngest boy, took a liking to the old warrior frog and transferred him to the Forge Pond, where he settled down and later we found him with quite a harem of lady frogs who bred in this pond. In the front gardens of the two-storey cottages was an old well, unused for many years, as the Company's water had been piped to the Thorne and the cottagers enjoyed the fruits of progress. Yet in my great-grandmother Pile's days this well had been the only means of getting water for drinking, bathing, and the week's washing. This well, like most wells, in time became the prison of frogs, newts and even grass snakes! By what my grandmother told me, and also my mother, was that it was nothing to see a couple of tadpoles slip out of the teapot into one's cup of tea, or for the spout to get blocked up by a newt or 'effet'!

It was after one of the periodical frog hunts that my Uncle Harry told us how he had been kept awake night after night at some place over in France in the 1914-18 War, by 'millions of frogs' in some ponds near a wood. Their croaking had been simply awful. Evidently afterwards, the Germans had attacked them, and for three days a terrible and bloody bayonet fight had been carried on for the possession of this wood. Anyway Uncle Harry's side had won, and kept the wood – and the questionable possession of the frog ponds as well!

It was at Pluckley Thorne, just down the road as it bends sharp left to Pluckley Pinnock, where the great snow-plough was kept when not in use. Nearly every winter it was called upon to clear the main roads and most-used lanes of snow. It was drawn by one or more horses according to the depth of snow to be cleared. In shape it was like a great triangle, made of thick, heavy boards and shod with iron at its apex or 'snout', with two long handles behind with which to help steer it. To see the snow-plough in action down the lanes, and to be able to follow it, always constituted a great occasion. The snow would be thrown forward and upwards to be piled on either side of the road or lane by the plough's action, very similar to that of a ship moving through the water and cutting through it with its sharp prow, sending the displaced element rippling away and outward.

\*\*\*\*\*\*

There had been times in the history of Pluckley School when complaints had been lodged with Mr Turff upon our conduct. Sometimes it was 'the Blackman boys' who were the culprits; sometimes 'the Beales' and 'that Fred Sanders'; at others 'Lemon-squash' Page from Lambden and my cousin Jim Pile of Hawthorn Cottage. Usually it was the Reverend Canon Springett DD, Mr 'Cocky' Evenden, 'Whiskers' Wood (of the forge on the hill), old Dicky Buss (the miller) or Mrs Crowcher (who lived at the top of Dicky Buss's Lane) who carried such complaints and sought redress of our 'gaffer'.

But when Gaffer Turff stood up one morning and made the announcement in morning-school that the Misses Maylam had reported to him that the Blackmans and the Luckhursts and quite possibly the 'Sanders boy' had broken nearly all the cloches, under which they propagated plants in their special small orchard opposite Mr Blackman's smithy, we-the-mentioned strenuously denied the accusation. The Rev. Canon Springett DD was called in. Both sides aired their views. We denied having thrown stones at what we called the 'glass-balls'. (Though we did not say that the stones we had flung at the fruit on the trees had fallen and accidentally smashed the 'closhers'.) The Maylam ladies left the school, still highly indignant, unappeased and unbelieving at not having been fully upheld by the headmaster and the 'fair play is a jewel' rector. Just before the reverend gentleman left, he turned to our headmaster and said: '*Qui n'entend qu'une cloche n'entend qu'un son*'. Old Gaffer pretended he knew what this meant but we knew better! Later, when I got home, I brought out my father's French dictionary and found it to mean, rather roughly translated, that people should always try to see both sides of a question.

Good old Canon!

\*\*\*\*\*\*

The old Pluckley football ground was opposite The Blacksmith's Arms at the Thorne. The field in which the pitch was situated belonged to Luckhurst House Farm just up the road towards Pluckley Hill. A well-known local sportsman and farmer by the name of Herbert Millgate – we always called him Bert – owned this property and took a great interest in the Pluckley Football Club. He had a fine flagpole put in the middle of the orchard between the field and the farmhouse from which he proudly flew the Union Jack, and on Saturdays when Pluckley was playing a home match, he would hoist the football club flag to fly below the Union Jack. This flag had on it the letters P.F.C. and he was responsible for getting it for the Club. People for miles around could see the football flag flying below the British flag and knew that Pluckley F.C. would be playing at the Thorne Ground during that particular afternoon. I always looked out for it from the fields at Mundy Bois a mile or more away. It was James Barry Blackman and his sons Ted ('Flannel') and Joe ('Blackie') who looked after the pitch, lined it out and erected the nets for the goals. This occupied Ted and Joe the best part of Saturday mornings. Joe was too young to play, but Ted was one of the regulars and a very good footballer.

Pluckley F.C. in the 1920s was an average team, though when they came up against such giants of the Ashford and District League like Tenterden, R.A.O.B. (Willesborough) and Ashford Working Men's Club, they usually ended up with anything from a six to ten goal defeat, playing as well and as hard as they could!

The home games with Ashford United and New Town Ramblers (from south Ashford) were always needle games, sometimes Pluckley just pipping them or they Pluckley. Ashford United were a very dirty-playing side and seemed to be composed mostly of the dealer and rag-

and-bone fraternity. Pluckley always had good and friendly games with Chilham, a clean-playing side and very sporting. I recall one terrific game in the Thorne Ground between Pluckley and Chilham, possibly in the 1922-23 season. A keen cold wind had been blowing nearly the whole of the game and one minute from time the teams were even, no goals having been scored. Suddenly the wind freshened and the clouds swept up from the Weald countryside and then, without warning, a hailstorm broke over the ground, blinding the players and stinging them through their skimpy clothing. Yet one Pluckley player had the ball and he ran on through the driving hail, it being in his back. The Chilham goalkeeper, half-blinded by the hailstones, ran out to intercept him just as the Pluckley forward shot for goal. The ball, a 'grass-cutter', swept along the ground and the goalie stopped to gather it just as a terrific flurry of hail hit him full in the face. He hesitated in his stoop, blinded by the storm, and missed the ball. It travelled between his legs and rolled slowly into goal to give Pluckley the game. As the referee blew for the goal, he looked at his watch and five seconds later he blew for full time, and this historic match was over!

There was one instance when Pluckley had a hard job to get a team together one Saturday, and James Barry Blackman turned out to play in goal. He was over fifty at the time. He did not have time to change into anything resembling football kit, so he played in his trousers, heavy boots, shirt and waistcoat! Very often I would play football in and around one of the goals with the Blackman and Luckhurst boys when the moon was at the full and the sky clear until half-past seven at night. It was eerie sport but very exciting and, of course, so different from playing in broad daylight.

Looking back on those good old times and the exploits of these men of Pluckley it is good to recall their names and to here append them as a memorial to their pluck and sportsmanship.

'Yet their names endureth.'

Mullins (who worked for Mr Buss, the baker at Pluckley)

Wicker (the village postman)

Joe Bodkin

Tom Morris (Metropolitan Police)

Barney Blackman (James Barry Blackman's eldest son)

Ted Blackman

Joe Blackman (who got his place in the team I think in the 1923-24 season)

James Barry Blackman (landlord of the Blacksmith's Arms)

Flying Officer Joliffe (RAF)

Flight Sergeant F. Sanders (my own father, in those days at RAF Records, Uxbridge)

Jack Henry

Tim Fidler (a son of Mr Fidler of the Black Horse inn at Pluckley Street)

Young Bert Millgate

Sidney Brown

Fred Tipples (who lived at Staplehurst)

One of two Mr Duncans (either Harry or George)

Charlie Wilcox

Mike Miles

Pluckley had a football club previous to the 1914-18 World War, though it ceased to exist until the 'boys came home' in 1919. Here for old remembrance are the names of the players of those days:

Captain Evan-Smith, Billy Francis, Charlie ('Tardy') Wilcox, 'Hibby' Wilcox, Mike Miles, Sam Miles, G. Robertson, 'Luck' Robertson, George Goodwin, Reg Draper, Alf East (P.C.), Martin (both of Ashford), Jack Foord, Charlie ('Snowball') Head, Fred Burrows (of

Charing), C. Bailey, George Gilbert, Sonny Clark, 'Brushy' Penticoat, Nat Miles and Ernest (Joe) Bodkin.

There were several gentlemen who took a great interest in those days in the welfare of the team, namely: the Rev. Canon Springett DD, Mr Moody-Smith, Mr Nelson, Percy Collins (landlord of the Dering Arms at Pluckley Station), Mr Walter Winans (the famous industrialist and big-game hunter), and Sir Henry Dering, Bart., of Surrenden.

In the 1920s those interested in the team were: the Rev. Canon Springett DD, Mr Herbert Millgate (of Luckhurst House Farm), James Barry Blackman (landlord of the Blacksmith's Arms), Sir Henry Dering, Bart., of Surrenden and Mr Duncan the haulage contractor at Chambers Green near Pluckley Station.

******

Old Rose Marchant's large cottage, set in a huge garden with many and varied fruit trees, was a great attraction to me and to my cousin Jim Pile who lived with his mother (my Aunt Fanny) at our grandfather's home, Hawthorn Cottage, just up the road from Old Rose's place. Her home was by Fir Toll, believed to be the site of a tollgate of the times of the highwaymen. Old Rose Marchant was a thick-set and wiry woman, who talked gruff like a man and worked like one too! We would often see her digging and weeding, quite tirelessly in her great orchard-cum-garden. In it grew every kind of vegetable, as well as the finest collection of old English garden flowers and medicinal herbs one would wish to see all at the same time.

Mr Marchant, her husband, always seemed a man in the background. Maybe old Rose made up for him with her voice and toughness. She had under her wing a niece, a lovely girl named Winnie, as fresh and graceful as a springtime morning. How old Rose would greet young

Jim and me! ''Ullo, young Jim; 'Morning, young Fred! Where be you two a-gooing? Up to some kind o' hanky-panky I'll be bound! Like some apples?'

If it wasn't apples, it would be pears, plums, gooseberries or redcurrants according to the season. She 'gave' us the old bullice tree (which bore lovely golden plum-like fruit) in the corner of her garden near the old stile. When the fruit was ripening we could go and help ourselves by standing on the top bar of the stile and pulling down the branches. Sometimes she would refer to us, individually, as in the case of Jim as 'Fanny's Boy' and myself as 'Alice's Eldest' (as I was my mother's eldest child).

It was the old stile near Rose Marchant's house, which opened the way to a narrow footpath leading away between her garden hedge and the ash tree plantation, that led Jim and myself on a voyage of discovery to find out where the pathway led. It was in the lovely autumn of 1919 and I was staying at my grandparents' at that time. When we got over the stile and followed the path it led us into a large square field, overgrown with great tussocks of coarse grasses and thickly populated with stinging-nettles and thistles. This spot, on account of its unkempt appearance, I named Jungle Field.

A right-o'-way led crosswise across this grassland from the old path from the stile. It came out onto the Malmains Road which led to the historic and ancient manor of Malmains. It was in this field that we found an old hoppers' kitchen that in the long-ago, when the parish of Pluckley had been about fifty per cent under acreage to hops, had supplied the means whereby the hop-pickers could heat water, cook food, and wash themselves. With the passing years it had gradually become a place where the gamekeepers of the Derings deposited old sacks, hen coops, broken boxes, feeding plates and china eggs, all useful things in the offices of breeding and looking after young pheasants. It was similar in build to the other old hoppers' building known as Brown's Kitchen over at Mundy Bois that had become a storage place for farm machinery on the land of Mr Strang of Greenhill Farm.

Jim and I, after exploring this exciting, musty and dusty place, and each pocketing a china egg for having fun with our schoolfellows later on, came out onto the Malmains Road and, crossing it, came to a sloping meadow just as rough and wild as the one we had left. This too was promptly given a name, it being that of Wild Field. This place had in it four ponds linked up by choked-up ditches and these pieces of water were full of weeds and their banks thick with razor-edged rushes. Many small scrubby thorn bushes also existed in and around them, and what with the long rank grass and the tough tussocks of the common rush, this field put me in mind of photographs of old and deserted gold-mine diggings of the Californian gold-rush era. Though no precious gold had been mined here, yet in some ways it was a 'diggings' of many years ago. The ponds had once been clay-pits from which had been taken clay for manufacturing bricks. These must have been used on the Dering estate and no doubt the clay was cut and the bricks produced by either some of the workmen of old Sir Edward Dering or his father.

At one end of this field was a large iron water-tank cart, its heavy metal wheels half-sunken in the clay soil. The water, which was seldom but a few inches from the brim, was maintained by the rains, and in this pond-on-wheels there resided many of the largest black water-beetles we had ever seen. How they came there was a mystery, though they might have been deposited there as eggs, brought in the beaks or on the feet of birds, from the margins of ponds in the vicinity. This water-tank cart became a happy play-place for us, and one new sport which we discovered by accident proved very popular with us. Jim had filled an old beer bottle with water and placed it in the ground, and I, with nothing much to do for a few moments had idly thrust a nut-stick into the open end of the bottle. This stick was a fairly neat fit, and as I drove it downwards into the bottle, the pressure caused some of the water to rush past the stick and squirted upwards into my face. Needless to say we tried this 'pushing the stick into the bottle and see what happens' game upon all our chums, much to our amusement!

In this wild and woolly meadow Jim and myself, aided by a friend named Lemon-squash Page from over at Snag's Mount Hill, played Red Indians. Armed with homemade bows and arrows we would stalk one another in the depressions and gullies, firing away with the element of surprise. Of course, this type of game palled as its excitement waned and we found a new use for our bows and our arrows. We would play at ambushing the 'stage-coach' from Denver, or Deadman's Gulch or whichever it might be. This was done by hiding behind the hedge and waiting for 'Pommer' Brown or 'Jumbo' Buss to come down the steep Station Road Hill from the eastern end of Pluckley village, and just as they got level with us Redskins we let fly our arrows into the front wheels of their cycles. Sometimes the arrows went harmlessly through, but now and again one would get caught swiftly up and as it revolved round would hit up hard against the mudguard stays or the top of the front wheel forks. This action halted the machine and the luckless rider ended up in the road!

But one fine frosty morning we met our Waterloo. Jumbo Buss came speeding down the last stretch of the hill, and he was ready for us. Just as we, hidden from sight, released our arrows, Jumbo braked his cycle to a skidding standstill, his grocer's basket half-leaping from the carrier in front. Our arrows sped into his stationary wheel and then he was over the hedge and after us! How we ran around that field, with Jumbo full of wrath not far behind us. We doubled back, throwing away our bows and arrows, and dived through the hedge into the road. Dashing past his recumbent cycle we disappeared into a narrow and tangly old wood opposite. But Jumbo crashed in after us, his great frame and weight sweeping aside the low boughs and bushes and, though we ducked and dived and evaded, he caught us one at a time and slammed home several ear-cracking slaps with his open ham-like hands around our unprotected craniums. How our ears whistled and our heads sang! 'That'll larn ye young devils!' he said, slapping his hands together and going out of the wood to remount his cycle. Warily we watched him out of sight round the bend at Rose Court and then, still rubbing our smarting ears and dizzy heads, went home to dinner much wiser than when we had started out that morning.

******

Up the hill road from California Field, on the way to the village, was Rectory Cottage, originally the Pluckley Rectory. When the Rev. Canon Springett came to the village his wife took over for her husband a lovely house with a park-like southern aspect. It was Mrs Springett who had the money and the fine rectory gave employment to several young women in the village as domestics, as well as a cook and a head gardener. Before my Uncle George joined the East Kent Regiment in the 1914-18 World War he was under-gardener there. During the early 1920s a Captain Money took over Rectory Cottage and after a bit of smartening up the name was changed to the more 'swanky' one of Greystones: as far as I was concerned this almost amounted to sacrilege, for certainly Rectory Cottage was a better name and in keeping with the village and its own surroundings.

Close by this house was a large pond in a long dell. It was a weed-clear piece of water in which many fine fish abounded. The deep dell ran up from this pond just off the Station Road Hill. It had very high and steep banks and was topped with giant horse chestnut trees, while below a variety of trees and brushes grew in confusion. Some said that this dell was a game-preserve for the cottage, and true, it always had a number of fine fat pheasants running in it, besides hares which seemed to like resting in the rough weeds and grasses covering the top-end slopes of the place. Yet I was never sure of this, for it seemed to me that this dell had been the source of quarrying in the long-forgotten past and that it had gradually become wooded over many generations; the large pond at the more open end of the dell being formed by the drainage of rainwater into it. In October the great trees alongside the road would cascade their smoothly gleaming dark brown horse chestnuts into the roadway and we boys could pick up hundreds of them with which to pelt the girls going to school, as well as using the finest and largest for our games of conkers.

At the top of this hill-road where it swung to the left to start the village street was situated close to the great double-iron gates of The Avenue, which led to the mansion of Surrenden Dering, a small square cottage called The Lodge. This was the gate-keeper's cottage, but old Mr Skeer had died many years ago and Sir Henry had let his widow continue to live there and carry out the functions of gate-keeper. She was an ill-tempered old woman, as near-looking to a witch as could be conjured up. In her reckoning of things it seemed that the Almighty came first, closely followed by Sir Henry Dering, with the Rev. Canon Springett bringing up the rear. All boys to her thinking should have been confined for ever in the regions of sulphur and fire.

She would watch Jim and me and shoo us away from the big gates as if we were everlasting sinners trying to sneak past the Golden Gates and into heaven undetected by the watchful St Peter. She would call us young rascals, scamps and miserable sinners. We would turn and call her 'Old Mother Skeer!' and then the fur flew. She would raise her skinny arms and shake her bony fists at us, threatening us with dire penalties from Above; from Sir Henry, the dear Canon, or Mr Turff the school-gaffer. 'I will tell't yer grand-fayther and grand-mither an ye!' she would shrill. We would reply that not only could she tell our grandparents but also our uncles and aunts, and Sir Henry Dering, Baronet! Then off we would run and to annoy her even more would climb onto the church wall nearby and run along it to the centre of the village street. The old maid had remarked to the Rev. Canon Springett: 'That them sarkie young'uns', 'sarkie' being the local dialect word for saucy, and the 'young'uns' she referred to being all boys in general!

Yet Jim and I often got through to Surrenden, for one of our schoolchums was young Bastin, the only child of Mr Bastin, Sir Henry's head-gardener. Though we never got any farther than the servants' entrance to the great mansion we could at least view this beautiful house in the golden days of summer or beneath a mantle of white in winter. Owing to a shortage of money Sir Henry and his family had not lived in the mansion in previous years, and he had leased it to the famous industrialist, sportsman and big-game hunter Mr Walter Winans. His coming to Pluckley had meant much to the village, in extra employment, and better still financially, for Mr Winans was a very liberal spender. He had some of the finest blood horses in his stables, and a wonderful herd of deer in Surrenden Park, besides some North American bison. He was game for anything from a pony-trotting race to hunting ghosts. He did sit up one night, so my grandfather told me, to try to lay the ghost of the White Lady who was reputed to haunt the great mansion. According to him he did encounter this famous county apparition, firing his revolver at her, the bullets passing through her wraithlike form as she disappeared through one of the walls of the big library.

Though Mr Winans had left Pluckley previous to 1919 when our family took up residence there again, his name was often in the news and I well remember the startling report in the *Daily Mail* when we were at our grandparents' house, that Mr Winans believed that in the depths of the unexplored hinterland of the African Congo that the great prehistorical Brontosaurus might still exist. Though arrangements were made for an expedition nothing further became of it.

Maybe it was the 'Walter Winans' fuel that helped to keep my own imagination burning in after years, as well as my later friendship with the late Cherry Kearton, another famous big-game hunter and also cinematographer, maker of several marvellous wild animal and jungle films. One of them was called *Dassan*. Anyway the lure of adventure and the unknown led me many years later into becoming a ghost-hunter or psychical researchist, and the explorer of 'Dead Man's Island' to wrench the secrets from its graveyard under the sea, and the hunt for a renowned prehistoric sea-reptile, a sort of miniature Plesiosaurus.

*To some, danger is not merely an inspiration; it is a thing necessary to their lives.*

*Some men must live uncomfortably, must seek out hardships and physical misery, in order to satisfy a yearning for a life that is different, and carries excitement before it.*

*Jungle Man* by Major P.J. Pretorius

# CHAPTER SIXTEEN

It was upon the Pluckley recreation ground that we lads learned to give and take knocks at cricket and football. On this fine piece of greensward our uncles also had been taught to 'play the game'. This wonderful playing field was given to the people and the children of Pluckley village by Sir Henry Dering of Surrenden, his finest gesture to our parish. It is still going strong and lies behind the north side of The Street, being flanked on the east and north by that one-time well-known landmark The Avenue, when it was bordered by its giant elm trees. The main Charing to Smarden round runs along its western side. Here on this playground Mr Turff our sporting headmaster coached and encouraged us. Many a 'needle' game of cricket did we boys of Pluckley School play against our old rivals the lads of Egerton, Charing and, in particular, Smarden schools. Two names from all those boys always stand out clear in my memory: Killick of Smarden and Newton-Clark of Charing, the finest spin bowlers it was every misfortune to have to play to! Yet we had some very good players at our own school but they were, sorrily, individualists who played to the gallery: Joe Blackman, 'Slogger' Tom Black, 'Curly' Goldup, Les Cooper and 'Captain' Clifton. The most sporting and useful cricketers we ever had were 'Sandy' Turner, young Homewood (the village butcher's eldest son) and Punch Luckhurst. Of my own prowess with the willow and ball little can be said except this remark: 'If there's no-one else to play, we'd better put him in!'

On this ground the Pluckley Cricket Club played its matches in the summertime against teams from Little Chart, Ashford, Hothfield,

Smarden, Charing, Bethersden, Great Chart and others. The heroes of
Pluckley were those giants of the flashing blade, Underwood and
Mullins. Underwood, who lived at Smarden, was the nearest approach
any amateur cricketer would hope to reach in comparison with that
magnificent Kent County Cricket Club player Frank Woolley; indeed,
Mr Underwood was known as the 'Village Woolley'. Mr Mullins was a
keen 'slogger' with an eagle eye for the rising ball. How we would
cheer when he knocked up such scores as thirty or over, composed
mostly of hits to the boundary for 'sixes'!

******

Pluckley Rookery began in some trees many generations before my
time. Form this nesting area of the great black and noisy rooks a row of
cottages opposite the south wall of the churchyard took their name:
The Rookery. The rooks, looked on as inhabitants of the village, were
never molested and so they built more and more nests, further and
further afield until they had spread to the great beech trees adown the
rectory drive nearby and to the stately elms of The Avenue where they
bordered the east side of the churchyard and the big recreation ground.
Not one of us lads, however venturesome and daring, ever took any of
the rooks' eggs, for the trees were unclimbable. You could get part of
the way up some of them and then the girth and formations of the great
boughs brought one to a halt, sometimes forty feet above the ground.

But it was good to hear the cawings and the scoldings of the rooks and
to watch them building nests or renovating old ones; to be able to
watch their twig-dwellings swaying in the north and north-east gales
and marvel at how they could stand up to such violently prolonged ill-
usage. Old Mother Skeer liked the rooks, for when they were busy at
their nest-building they would drop far more nesting material to the
ground than they used, and it was an easy job for this ancient dame

from the lodge-keeper's cottage to fill her apron over and over again with fine twigs to stack by with which to light her winter fires.

Perhaps one of the most interesting places in the village was the Dering Vault, situated under the Dering Chapel, itself a part of Pluckley Church. This burial chamber was filled to bursting-point with the coffined remains of the great Dering family of Surrenden Dering, going back for hundreds of years. To this vault there belonged a wonderful legend as told to me by my grandfather Jesse Pile, a rare teller of tales. Several hundred years ago, so his father had told him, and he his father before him, a beautiful Lady Dering had died. She was the apple of her young husband's eye and her death brought him to untold grief. Before the lovely maiden who had been his wife was finally shut into the dark of the old vault he had her dressed in her finest dress and in her crossed hands he placed a blood-red rose, symbol of their love. Then the corpse was placed in an airtight lead sheating, and round this were placed six more coverings of lead. And, continued my grandfather, if her coffin ever be opened by mortal man, she will be just as lovely and fair as she was when they laid her to rest hundreds of years ago! Truly a most wonderful and lovely story. It is said that at night her ghost can be seen haunting the old churchyard. Certainly a spectre no-one could be afraid of meeting!

It was when the steeplejacks arrived in Pluckley one fine morning that we boys really began to take an interest in the church of St Nicholas where so many of our parents had been married and so many of us had been baptised. The wooden shingles covering the ancient spire were to be taken off and new ones put on. Our headmaster was just as interested in what was going on up aloft as his scholars, and it would be hard to say whether the schoolchildren spent more time tying to glimpse the steeplejacks during lessons, or our head Mr Henry Edwin Turff! He explained to us how deceptive distances can be in relation to the size of objects, and illustrated this by pointing out the large panels in the doors of the school store cupboard being of the same area as the wood shingles, which looked no larger than the tops of matchboxes upon the steep sides of the tapering steeple. After those wonderful people, the steeplejacks, had finished their work and left the village, word got round that Tom Black had shaken hands with one of them! This we could not believe! We knew he had shaken hands with the French airmen who had been forced down on the old landing ground at Pluckley Ley; we knew he had shaken Mr Mullins' hand when he scored thirty runs at cricket in one over; we knew he had shaken hands with many drivers of the giant traction engines; yet we would not take it to us that he had been so highly honoured as to have shaken the hand of such a personage as a *steeplejack*!

It was rumoured that at various times he had been picked out to be patted upon the shoulder by Colonel Cheeseman of Chart Court; that Sir Henry Dering had even patted him upon his barbed-wire hair head, and that Walter Winans had spoken to him when he was pushed around in a pram! 'That might be true,' remarked my chum Bob Beale, 'if they had a pram big enough to carry his head in!'

******

The actual village of Pluckley is situated in its parish near to the northern boundary, not far from the parish of Little Chart. The Street, as its main thoroughfare is called, is more of a wide square than anything, with its continuation running to where the road sweeps right opposite to the old cottage of the ancient Mother Skeer. Down to my grandfather's middle years – he died when he was eighty-five years old – an annual fair was held in this square or street, with many stalls selling all kinds of things, such as sugar-pigs, gilt gingerbread, coloured rocks and other toothsome eatables; cheap jewellery figured prominently, and ladies' favours, lucky heather, dolls and love potions for the village swains; there would also be a Punch and Judy show, and an organ-grinder with a red-fuzzed monkey atop his organ which was supported upon a single leg like a one-legged fisherman with his sole remaining 'leg' made of polished wood. There would be coloured streamers, balloons and ladies' ticklers on sale, as well as Jews' harps, penny tin whistles and oranges. There was much dancing and prancing as the evening grew on and night descended. Tin whistles, gipsy tambourines, drums and accordions would supply the music for the dancers. Everywhere would be movement, colour, lights and laughter, mixed with saucy badinage and the high shrill cries of the girls being coaxed, kissed and tickled by the males indulging in this annual 'free-for-all' gathering.

Actually the old village street had run up across the great square, past the Black Horse inn to where on one side stood the old coaching house and stables of the inn, and two cottages. Opposite these a row of cottages extended to the church gate, the last cottage being that of a former village bakers, to which was attached the original bakehouse. Next to the Black Horse was the headmaster's house covered with ivy and its main garden atop of a twelve foot wall of ragstone which swept round the corner from The Street to the road from Smarden to Charing. At the eastern end of The Street were the extensive outbuildings of the village builder, carpenter and undertaker, in those days a Mr Turner. Then working back came the famous old Fig Tree Cottages with its giant fig-tree, followed by the entrance to the long downhill drive to the rectory of Canon Springett. Next came the saddler's wooden workshop to which was attached the local branch of the free County Library presided over by a happy little lady named Mrs Button, whom it was my pleasure to help, at certain times, in the selection of books from the large motor-van that brought new volumes and took away those that had been read. Then came the row of very fine houses or cottages known as the Rookery Cottages. The village school came after, with its small bell tower and hand-sounding bell; then the outbuildings and slaughterhouse and yard of the village butcher Mr George Homewood and his own house and shop.

Facing the length of the street was the village stores, presided over at various times by Mr Cornes (of the Cornes Brothers, well-known shopkeepers and farmers in our district in years gone by), Mr Evenden, and the Lewis & Co. The Stores, as this general shop was called, sold everything, and it was always my great delight, when on holiday at my grandparents', to go 'up The Street to the shop' with my grandmother to help with the shopping. For my help I was always awarded with two ounces of sugar-coated pear-drop sweets by my grandmother. The sweet scent from these sweetmeats, as I sucked them, blended with the aromas of pepper, vinegar, oranges, apples, cheese and bacon which always pervaded the atmosphere in this wonderful village shop. This blend of accumulated scents and aromas left in my mind unforgettable memories. In this rambling general store had worked, over the years, Mr Evenden, Mr Brissenden, Pommer Brown, my Uncle Ted (Edwin Pile), a pre-1914 Territorial who had been one of the first of our soldiers sent overseas to India, and later he had died gallantly upon a desert battlefield in the Persian Gulf area fighting the Turks. The last letter he ever wrote home contained these words: 'We are soon going out to the battlefield, trusting in God and believing in our cause...' Not many hours afterwards this handsome and brave young uncle of mine had laid down his life in the cause of Freedom. Bill Luckhurst, who lived at Fir Toll, had been employed in this establishment and Jumbo Buss at one time had been an errand-boy there. Many of the boys and girls who had left Pluckley School had found their first jobs there. Jumbo of my generation was one of them; Miss Connie Filmer was another. A dark-haired country beauty, a Miss Jarvis from Bethersden, had been employed in the Post Office which was incorporated in the Stores. She had left to marry, and make a good match with, 'Sonny' Evenden, only son of Mr Evenden, who had had a lovely modern-style house built in a very pleasant situation near to Ragged House Farm at Kingsland, Egerton. Attached to the store premises were those of the baker of those days, old Mr Buss, whose bakery was beneath his house, the entrance to the bakehouse being on Pluckley Hill. For him worked Mr Mullins, one of the cricketing and footballing 'stars' of our parish.

At this bakery one of our schoolmates worked, before he even left school. This was Fred Watts, who lived near Chart Court with his sister and widowed mother. He was a true young Briton, working during his off-times and holidays from school – while we other lads played or rambled the fields and lanes – to help keep his mother and the home together. He was a hard-working, happy and contented lad, a page out of Life's copybook to us other boys. After he left school he was given regular and full-time employment on the estate of Sir Henry Dering as his milkman. One thing I can always say of the Derings is that they looked after the people whom they employed. They never let them down: they helped them to the best of their abilities as became the wide separation between them, as the gentry, and the artisans they employed.

There is little doubt that the Tuckshop, as it was called, perched upon its high pavement almost opposite to Mr Buss the baker's place, was the one shop we schoolchildren held dear to our hearts. Here the amiable and very ladylike Mrs Jennings presided over her many kinds of sweets in large bottles. Here we purchased our marbles, fishing lines, fish-hooks, whip and peg tops, tin whistles and non-alcoholic drinks. Mostly we smoked Park Drive at 4d for 10 cigarettes as we were saving this firm's cards, such as 'Animals and Birds of Commercial Value', 'Plants of Commercial Value' and 'Aesop's Fables'. In summer we drank refreshing lemonades; in winter we imbibed hot blackcurrant or cherry. What big fellows we felt as we drained our glasses to the dregs, or puffed and coughed over our 'gaspers'!

******

One Sunday during the summer of 1923 I arrived at Prebbles Hill Farm to be met by Bob Beale with a wonderful tale of a place where he and his brother John had been to the previous day. 'It's way over there,' said he, pointing across towards Charing some four miles distant. He told of sandpits they had found and some birds like swallows that lived in them. Also they had come across some wonderful flowers never seen before. So it came about that the following Saturday we would all go over to this new countryside exploring. I met the Beales at their farm and with a haversack filled with sandwiches and a large bottle of water, we set off soon after dinner. Our way went by Kingsland to the turnpike, and past Chart Court and the ancient church of Little Chart. Along the main Pluckley to Charing road we rambled, passing the quiet rectory of the Reverend Hill until we came to a branch lane on the left leading through the chestnut woods. 'We go down here' said Bob, and down we went. This was Newlands Lane, where on the right-hand side stood a farm called Hunger Hatch. This place, in much later years, became the home of the famous stage star Jeanne de Casalis. At the end of this lane we came into another roadway. A signpost informed us that we had come from Pluckley and Little Chart; that if we went left we should reach a place called Barnfield and if we went right we should arrive at Charing Heath. 'Which way?' I asked Bob. 'To the right' said he, and to the right we went.

I had heard of Charing Heath before: a place of old winding lanes, mostly cut deep through sandstone hills impregnated with a form of ironstone, called by local people 'lightning stone' because they presumed that lightning had run to earth in these parts and fused the sand into iron! The sandy hills were to the north, though the central and southern parts were wild, flat countryside. We soon came upon two small sandpits: one disused; the other being quarried. It was here that Bob and John proudly showed me the mysterious flowers. I was enchanted, for I had never seen such before. They were foxgloves, the wild reddish variety with the brown snakish markings. I gathered some of these treasures to take home to astound my neighbours. Later that year I found some more out on Hothfield Common. Two years later some more came to light in the woods along the old Bowl Road leading from the top of Charing Hill to the Bowl Inn near Stalisfield. These three places were the only ones in which I ever discovered the elusive foxgloves growing, around these particular districts. We entered the woods hereabouts on Charing Heath and found them drenched with humidity. In the cleaner places we came across thistles growing eight feet high and the pinkish flowering wood orchids reaching two feet high, their exceptional growth being due to the warmth and moisture held captive in these marshy tracts of woodland. Also, the sandy soil below the thin subsoil may have helped by making these plants drive their roots deeper. Where the trees shadowed stretches of these lanes cut through the higher parts of the heath, and where the breeze blew along these 'tunnels', the atmosphere was beautifully cool and it was amongst the waving grasses upon the lane-side banks that we found the delicate blue harebells flowering. Only on Charing Heath, along such lanes as these, could they be discovered. Suddenly our lane came into another road. A signpost pointed from whence we had come: Little Chart and Barnfield. To our right it said Charing: to our left Charing Heath and Egerton, and pointing a finger up a tiny gravelled lane opposite to us it conveyed the message 'To Kenmore'. 'Never heard of it,' said Bob. 'Nor me!' replied John, and I had to confess to being as ignorant as they about Kenmore. So we crossed the main roadway and went to seek Kenmore. We found a vast stretch of poultry farming land with a large modern house. This was a scientific poultry farm wondrous to see, run by the Kenmore Egg Farm Limited, with its fine buildings and thousands of cleanly looking chickens. Less than a year later I got to know this farm well as I went to learn under the Biggs Brothers of Roundwood Scientific Poultry Farm, perched 600 feet above sea level in the North Downs above Charing. Later I came down to manage for Captain Barbrooke, at Swan Street Poultry Farm, his complete laying stock of some 2,000 birds, Kenmore and Swan Street being neighbours on the Heath. This was early in 1925 when I was not yet seventeen.

From Kenmore we wandered back to the main highway and turned towards the village of Charing Heath, passing on our way, on the top of a hill, a large sandpit used for occasional quarrying. Here we saw, set in the upper face of the sand quarry, scores of little holes, the entrances to the tunnels into the sands at the ends of which the swallow-like sand martins built their bits of nests, laid eggs and raised their young. For quite a long time we watched the comings and goings of these birds. What with the sandpits, the giant orchids and thistles; the foxgloves, harebells and the Kenmore Egg Farm, plussed on to these squeaking, restless birds, our cap of exploration seemed brim full. Yet we had other wonderful things ahead of us. Passing through the quiet village the people about looked hard at us, for we were real strangers to them – 'foreigners' is the word! Then up a long steady hill, until we arrived at the top. Here Bob exclaimed 'I know where we are now! This farm here is La Trobes'. Yes, this was Brockhill Farm, and we had just climbed Brockhill. The La Trobes were two

Frenchmen who had come over here to farm after the end of the 1914-18 war. One lived in the large old Brockhill Farm, while his brother had a new place – a maison, not a farm – a little way down a side-road going to Lenham Heath. It was the little boy and girl and their dog who often shouted after me when I was newsboy for Mr Moody the newsagent at Charing, for I delivered the news all over Charing Heath, part of Lenham Heath, Egerton Green, Egerton village to Egerton Forstal and Mundy Bois. They would stand right in the middle of the road with their arms wide apart to try to make me get off my cycle, but I always eluded them with a swerve to the left or right. Then they would call after me *'C'est un petit cochon! Petit cochon! Petit cochon!'* which being translated meant 'He is a little pig – little pig – little pig!' They would call to their little dog to run after me to bite my *jambes* but the dog could never be persuaded and I would leave them far behind scolding him for his cowardice.

So Bob, John and I went in the direction of Egerton along the long flat road from Brockhill Farm. Later we arrived at a steep and narrow lane leading to a drunken-looking signpost indicating to Barnfield. 'We go down here!' called Bob, but the main highway continued from here and swept steeply down between a high-banked wood on one side and a very high bank on the other. This looked much more inviting, for this led to new territory. Stonebridge Green said the signpost, and also indicated that Egerton village was a mile and a half distant across, to us, unexplored country. So we decided not to go over to Barnfield, but to Stonebridge Green.

As we passed down the tree-shaded road we saw to our left, perched high on the steep bank, a picturesque old house, with sloping gardens filled with all kinds of old English garden flowers. This place was, I later learned, the home of Mrs Lake, a teacher up at Egerton School. At the bottom of the steep hill the road split up: one lane led left and the other went to Lenham Heath. We took the left to Egerton. Soon we came around this winding lane to a great sheet of water, known as the Mill Lake. Upon its tranquil surface swan several lovely swans. In the distance was a wooded and very swampy island, which a year or two later I discovered was the resting-place of several pairs of grebes. A humpbacked bridge carried the road over an underground tunnel through which water was run to regulate the height of water in the lake. There was a sluice gate on one side of the bridge behind a high board fence. On the other we could look down to the water cascading out of the tunnel under the road and watch a pair of lovely yellow wagtails flitting quietly about below. This was the first time I had encountered these rather rare birds. Adown the down, when we had crossed the bridge we found the Egerton watermill and its giant fascinating wheel. Soon afterwards we arrived at Stonebridge Green, a place so often referred to as Egerton Green. Here we found a real green, forming a large and verdant triangle. A few large houses, a short row of small country cottages and The Good Intent inn formed the human side of this quiet piece of countryside.

So this, I thought, is Stonebridge Green, where, according to old Mr Charlie Cuthbert who lived at Mundy Bois, one of his sporting sons in the very long ago had fought for three-and-a-half hours against the 'Ashford Terror'. It was the last great bare-knuckle fight at Egerton. The Ashford Terror who had challenged 'Battling Cuthbert' on his home ground was knocked out after a terrific battle which commenced at eight o'clock in the evening and ended at eleven-thirty, oil lamps having been lit to provide illumination on the Green. This great fistic encounter must have taken place in the early nineteen-hundreds.

******

When old Mr Turk sold his farm, Little Mundy Bois, around 1921, another farmer called Mr Luckhurst came there from Great Chart. He had two sons and a grown-up daughter and the coming of two more lads to Mundy Bois was well-heralded by myself and brothers, as it meant more fun and company in our games and play. The elder boy, Harry, was a good cricketer and footballer and his younger brother Jack a very keen and forceful player. Harry, who was near school leaving age at that time, helped his father about the farm a great deal of the time and mostly milked the two cows they owned. These were milked in a bow-byre forming part of the outbuildings to Appleby Grange, and my brothers and I very often went to watch Harry doing the milking and be given copious drinks of steaming warm milk straight from the udders. How creamily warm and smoothly delicious was that milk direct from the cows to our greedy little stomachs! In the old cow-byre, several swallows had their open-topped mud nests up on the beams, and came and went, feeding their hungry youngsters as if such things as boys and cows had never existed.

Across the road was the fine old Tudor manor house, Mundy Bois Farm (Big Mundy Bois we called it, to differentiate between the Big and Little Mundy Bois Farms). Here lived Captain Leonard Slaughter and his magnificent wife: magnificent of figure, looks and voice. They had no children of their own, and never did have any. Perhaps because of this, the Slaughters always gave us lads – my brothers and the two Hart boys – the run of their farm, farmyard and the great pond situated in it. 'Such sweet little dears' she called us, though it must have been quite evident to her that we were just as 'holy little terrors' as well. Though the Slaughters were always held in the highest esteem by us, we never really forgave them for what transpired from one incident that, quite possibly, could have turned out tragically, yet which ended by being the greatest laugh Mundy Bois ever had.

It happened this way. It was during the summer of 1922, and one Saturday afternoon the two Hart boys, Cyril and Cecil, and two of my three brothers Wallie and Ted, and myself, had gone to spend the afternoon paddling in the large farmyard pond at Mundy Bois Farm. We had been thoroughly enjoying ourselves for some time until Ted, who was seven years old at the time, decided to go into the water at a spot where I had warned him not to. It was dangerous on account of the slope under the water. This slope, composed of the Weald clay, was hard and very slippery under the water and soon had one upon their back, and immersed. That is what happened to Ted. I heard a slither and a splash. Turning, I saw Ted upside-down in the pond some feet from the edge, with his legs sticking up in the air. Wading quickly out I grabbed his ankles, swung him around and dragged him out feet first. As it happened, as if by a miracle he had kept his mouth shut – for a change! – and had swallowed no water. He was hustled off to an empty pigsty that was clean and full of fresh straw. He was stripped naked and covered all over in the warm straw except for his head. His jersey, shirt, shorts, stockings and boots were disposed upon the sloping corrugated iron roof of the sty where they were dried by turning them from time to time, over and over in the broiling mid-afternoon sunshine. Just as his clothes were judged dry and were being taken off the roof Mr and Mrs Slaughter chanced by. Of course they wanted to know what was going on and I had to very reluctantly tell them what had happened. 'Oh, the poor dear little thing!' exclaimed Mrs Slaughter in her beautifully modulated and cultured voice, as she peeped into the pigsty to observe young Ted surrounded with straw in a far corner. After getting Ted dressed we left for home. As we went away Mrs Slaughter exclaimed to Captain Slaughter: 'But how really priceless!' Anyway, when we got home we said 'nowt' and passed muster. That evening my father came home on leave from the RAF Depot at Uxbridge and the next morning we were soon 'on parade'.

He had been told by Captain and Mrs Slaughter about the pond-and-pigsty incident. 'This is it,' I thought, 'I'm the eldest and I'll get the hiding.' But the incident passed off: perhaps the humour of this exploit had softened my strict parent's heart; on the other hand, if I had been thrashed the Slaughters might have got to hear of it and they would have felt responsible for 'telling on us' as we phrased tales of our 'lawful occasions' which got to the ears of our parents, or others. No doubt they were correct in speaking about the incident to our father, yet our rigid schoolboy code of not 'telling tales' rebelled against such a thing. For a long time we banned the Slaughters' farm and would not play on it, and I even gave a very cold 'Good-day' to the Slaughters when I encountered them out.

It was during this eventful summer that word got around Mundy Bois by way of Arthur Collins that he had seen a large golden bird near the crossroads just inside the outskirts of the old Smarden Forest (or the Dering Wood, as it is unromantically named on the Ordnance Survey maps). Did I know what sort of bird it could be, I was asked. My reputation as a juvenile naturalist was at stake. 'It might be a yellow wagtail,' I replied evasively, though I knew it could not be. So off I went down the long straight road to the Devil's Bush in the middle of the crossroads and watched from there the surrounding forest. Many birds came and wet, but no golden-looking bird. Tiring of my lone vigil I was about to quit the shelter of the clump of trees and bushes named after the sulphurous 'Old Nick' when I heard the flap of wings and, glancing up and across the road, saw just settling upon a branch, high up in a tree, the mysterious bird. Yes, it was golden all right! Such a bird I had never seen before in this district; only as a colour plate in a book. It was a golden oriole, and I could not get back to our hamlet fast enough to proudly present its inhabitants with the astounding news. My stock rose considerably and never dwindled from that momentous day.

****** 

After I left school in 1922, and before I went into regular employment to learn the art of scientific poultry farming, I had a lot of time on my hands which was divided up between scouring the countryside in search of natural history and the carrying-out of many small odd jobs for Mrs Cooper at the Rose and Crown, Mrs Slaughter at Mundy Bois Farm, Mrs Duncan at Little Mundy Bois Farm, as well as Captain Pinkney of Appleby Grange and the Scottish farmer Mr Strang up at Greenhill. With some of the money from these many and varied employments I was able to at last purchase for myself books, at modest prices, in the town of Ashford to which I walked before my father gave me a bicycle to have for my very own. My library had commenced with a volume by Patterson called *Zoology for Schools*, very well illustrated with woodcuts, many of them being skeletal and anatomical, from the *Infusoria* way up to *Bimana*. It was with the aid of these anatomical woodcuts that I practised upon the dead bodies of grass snakes, frogs and birds. If anyone killed a rabbit or chicken in our hamlet they gave me the entrails to 'play with' as well as their heads if they did not want them. I purchased *Zoology for Schools* from Rusty Blackman of The Street at Pluckley for fourpence and half a bag of bull's-eyes: I shall always consider it to have been my greatest buy in those faraway days. Then I purchased, at the book and shoe repairers' shop in Station Road, Ashford, a very nice volume of Gilbert White's fascinating *Natural History of Selbourne* for the great sum of sixpence. This old boot repairer, a well-read man, sold secondhand books as a sideline and this made his shop the most fascinating boot repairing shop in the whole wide world – excepting that of Mr Woodcock at Pluckley Thorne where I went regularly each week to read his *Police News*, a blood-spattered and horrific weekly paper that made one's hair stand on end!

Then came other additions to my library of natural history. For twopence I bought the Reverend J.G. Wood's *Common Objects by the Sea-shore* at our local jumble (or rummage) sale during November 1922, following this with two new books purchased in Ashford the next spring. These were Gallichan's *Birds and their Nests and Eggs and how to identify them* and, by another author, *Inhabitants of the Seashore and How to find them*. How wonderfully happy and knowledgeable I felt with those fine books.

Two of the books I still have, precious possessions, hard-earned as a lad over forty years ago. They have a proud place among the hundreds of works I now own on zoology, botany, geology, and other branches of the world of Nature: they are *Zoology for Schools* and *Natural History of Selbourne*. Many years later I came to pay a pilgrimage to this famous village and the places dear old Gilbert White wrote about during his rectorship back in the 18<sup>th</sup> century.

*In the little crimson manual 'tis written plain and clear*
*That who will wear the scarlet coat will say goodbye to fear;*
*Shall be a guardian of the right, a sleuth-hound on the trail.*
*In the little crimson manual there's no such word as fail;*
*Shall follow on though Heaven falls, or Hell's top turrets freeze,*
*Half round the world, if need there be, on bleeding hands and knees.*
*It's duty — duty first and last, the crimson manual saith;*
*The scarlet rider makes reply: 'It's duty to the death';*
*And so they sweep the solitudes, free men from all the earth.*

'Clancy of the Mounted Police', by Robert W. Service

# CHAPTER SEVENTEEN

Many have been the times that I have stood at the top of Greenhill where its narrow lane leads to the Top Road linking Egerton with Pluckley, and gazed out across the Charing Valley to the high North Downs shutting off the northern countryside from mid-Kent and the lovely Weald. Though I had often walked to Charing to buy from Mr Moody's shop such glorious boys' weeklies as *The Magnet*, *Boys' Realm* and others, yet I had never ventured north and beyond that large and busy village. No doubt on account of the time, for it was a five-and-a-half mile walk to Charing and by the time we had got there it was time to turn back towards distant Mundy Bois.

Yet eventually I did make a lone expedition to that high range of green slopes, beset with wild woods and old chalk quarries. Heading north out of Charing, I plodded up the main road which goes caterwise over Charing Hill, part of the Downs, until I reached the old Clock House. A narrow lane, unmetalled, turned off to the left here; this lane being part of the ancient Pilgrims' Way running from Winchester to Canterbury, the route of devout Christians of old times who made pilgrimages to Canterbury Cathedral. Before their time, no doubt, the invading Romans had used this route to set near the foot of the Downs. Possibly before the Romans the Ancient Britons had used it as a high dry road. Though the animal life of these highlands was similar to that of the lower country, the plant life was absolutely different in many ways. Here I discovered the delicate yellow rock roses growing, and the wild thyme or marjoram. How wonderful was the aromatic scent this thyme diffused into the atmosphere! The sprawling golden carpets

made by the millions of flowers of the birds' foot trefoil made me catch
my breath in wonderment. Another flower peculiar to these Downs
was the yellow wort. Here on these chalky uplands as summer
progressed could be discovered many orchids: Twayblade, Pyramidal,
Man orchids, Bee and White Heleborine. Foxes and rabbits abounded
here, the former living upon the latter. Fine sparrowhawks hovered
over the green slopes and the woods watching for the fieldmice, baby
rabbits, birds and voles. Robber rooks flew here from the old rookery
attached to Clearmont House on the lower Charing Hill road, not to
hunt for wild game for their nestlings but for young chicks and ducks in
this downland farm and rickyards, and to steal eggs from nests which
they had observed where some of the fowls 'laid away' under the
hedgerows and bushes away from the farms.

On these North Downs above Charing it was the survival of the fittest
and especially so in the case of the rabbits, though their fast breeding
always more than made up for the losses of the rabbit population
caused by the never-ending attacks and killings of the many foxes. At
the very summit of the high ground, in one corner of a very large and
wandering stretch of land of many corners, I stumbled upon a dew
pond which got its supply of water mainly from the mists and the
dews. A couple of oak trees, the branches of which overhung the
shallow depression, condensed the molecules of water in the
atmosphere and from the leaves and branches the drops of dew-water
fell incessantly into the pond. Even in the severe drought of 1921,
when all the Charing valley ponds and most of those in the Weald
dried out, this small pond, perched six hundred feet above sea level,
retained water sufficient for the wild animals and birds living in its
vicinity. Later, this piece of downland country became known as
Roundwood Scientific Poultry Farm, and happily, to which after I had
left school I went to learn this most interesting trade, leaving it after

becoming a fully-fledged scientific poultry farmer for the excitement and variety of newspapers and ink. These downlands had many old chalk quarries left like giant pockmarks upon their faces, in which one could chip out endless fossil remains such as shells and the spines of sea-urchins. In the red clay that formed the thin covering over the chalk, many fossil spongers could be brought to light and the most fantastically-shaped flintstones one could wish to have.

Another lone expedition was when I left Mundy Bois one sunny after-dinner time to walk to Ashford some nine miles away. I went through Little Chart and reached Hothfield and its wild and interesting heathland and the famous Hothfield Bog where many sheep and cows had met a dreadful doom. Here grew the marsh orchids and, so some said, the lizard orchids. In later years I spent many happy hours exploring this great heath and the bog from all kinds of flowers as well as the orchids, and discovering several birds and plants we could not boast of having in our own parish of Pluckley and the hamlet of Mundy Bois. Eventually I reached Ashford town and struck south to a place called Beaver. Pushing on I got lost in the fields around Kingsnorth and then picked up the Great Stour river. This I followed back north in the hopes of getting to the main London-to-the-coast railway lines to pick up my bearings. Somehow or other I misplaced this river and followed one of its affluents which came down to join it from Repton. This large stream went under a girdered bridge over which the permanent way was carried. The stream was too deep to wade so I hauled myself hand-over-hand by the lower flange of one of the great T-bar girders. Halfway over an express train thundered by overhead making my fingers dance dangerously upon the ironwork. Anyway I got over safely. Northwards the land was dense with trees and rank vegetation as far as I could see. So I crossed the railway lines and went south with an idea in my mind. I tried to locate the over two-hundred-foot chimney shaft of the Pluckley Brick and Tile Words near Pluckley Station about five miles down the line. At last I saw it, thin and friendly in the far distance, and then made for it 'as the crow flies'. Over ditches, hedges and fields until at last I reached Pluckley. Crossing the railway again I headed for home – and food! For I had been without anything to eat for eight-and-a-half hours. Only a few mouthfuls of water from the Great Stour had I partaken. Yet food in such adventures never entered my head, as long as I could get a good drink of clean water to break my thirst.

******

Many and varied were the games we played at Pluckley School. The rougher the better! 'Bombardment' was one of these, when one set of lads bombarded (they being the 'field gun' and crews) with lumps of ragstone the 'infantry' at the other end of the playground. One had to be very nippy to avoid injury in this game. 'Convicts and Warders' was another game we loved when the 'convicts' escaped from their 'prison' (the school lobby) and had fights with the 'warders' who tried to get them back into 'prison'!

Then there were such games as 'Mustard and Cress', 'Sparking', 'Tin can football' and 'Old Gal'. Like most country schools in these days, during the summertime it became Zoological Gardens on a small scale: as we brought into school as pets whatever we had captured in our hour-and-a-half's lunchtime break. Grass snakes and slow-worms; all kinds of young birds like blackbirds, thrushes, wrens, robins, moorhens, jays and many others. Frogs, newts, moles and field voles were common company, and now and again a hedgehog was brought in to cause a diversion from lessons. How our long-suffering headmaster Mr Turff kept his hands and cane off us I cannot think, yet he seemed to take it all in good part.

It was always in the autumn when the marble season began at Pluckley School and wherever one looked this game could be seen in progress. In October 1921 I organised a Marbles Championship which, after a bitter battle, I won by beating Ron Haffenden by 69 hits to 68. The course was from the top of Dicky Buss's Lane to the front gate of the Misses Maylam's house (once a farm) at Pluckley Thorne. This course was roughly along three-quarters of a mile of broad macadamised road and lent itself to long throws and fast-moving play. The trouble-spot was halfway down Pluckley Hill where this particular autumn, after a lot of rain, springs broke out upon this hill road and, owing to the passage of many muddy-wheeled carts, this particular section got thick with gritty mud of the gluey nature. Here the marbles got bogged down and the games degenerated into brute force and trust-to-luck! Eight of us paired off for the first round, making a semi-final of the next round with two pairs, the winning semi-finalists being the pair to fight out the final. Those who took part being, as I have mentioned, eight in number, were as follows: Punch Luckhurst, 'Tucker' Luckhurst, Ern Luckhurst; 'Nibs' Blackman and 'Blackie' Blackman; Ron Haffenden; my brother Walter Sanders and myself.

Anything in the sporting line I went in for, from playing my uncle Walter Pile at draughts to playing cricket and football for the village school. In the top-spinning season I spent hours slashing a whip-top along the roads and lanes and once set myself the terrific task of whipping a top from Pluckley Thorne down to The Pinnock and then on to the crossroads at Mundy Bois. This I achieved but only with luck, for my firmly-knotted whip gradually wore itself down and down until I had to hit, with more luck than judgement, on the very last lap from the Rose and Crown inn to the crossroads, the wobbling green top with only two inches of string and the tip of the stick. The distance was nearly one-and-a-half miles, and whipping a top over such a length was never equalled in our parish or those around it. No doubt on account of no-one else being such a chump as to try to do such a thing! Perhaps my best sporting achievements were at football and cricket: at football, sharing the honours of many a rearguard action with my friends Punch Luckhurst and 'Penny' Pentecost who lived near Pluckley Station. We made the finest half-back line Pluckley School ever had, and I am sure has never had since: Pentecost as left-half, Punch as centre-half and I as right-half. However big they came we tricked and eluded them: never was a forward-line fed so well with the ball as was ours! We never scored any goals but we helped to make them. The only time I ever scored a goal was when playing right-back for the Pluckley Youths' Football Club, formed at the start of the 1923-24 season, and which collapsed before that footballing season ended. It was composed of a 'rebel' element who could not get places in the regular Pluckley Football Club team and some of us who had not been left school more than a year: the rebels being Tom Black, Joe Blackman and one of the Smith boys from Kingsland. Our first match was away to a team of Smarden youths and they plastered us with goals to the tune of nineteen to nil, five minutes before full-time. Suddenly our side woke up and Ozzie Rice raced nearly the length of the field to score and reduce the deficit. From the midfield kick-off Smarden's forwards swept down and, slashing ball, sped goalwards: the Kingsland Smith right out of position. In an effort to save the goal I kicked as the ball flashed by me. It only caught the tip of my left boot and this seemed to add more impetus to it as it crashed into the net. 'That's it!' yelled Blackman, Black and Smith together, 'Go on, score for the other side!' To which I replied that it was nearly time that some of our side scored a goal or two, and they couldn't say I hadn't netted the leather. That was the last goal of that debacle and we went home to Pluckley well and truly licked!

Yet I had, in my last year at school, brought fame to our cricketing side and covered myself with glory. Smarden School had a long innings to score 68 runs. Pluckley School were 38 for 9 wickets, and I was last man in. Young Stan Turner had carried his bat as one of the opening pair and was at the wicket with 28 runs to his credit. 'Block 'em!' hissed Stan as I passed him, 'and leave the runs to me!' By luck I did manage to 'block 'em' that first over. Stan then had the bowling and he played the wily Killick with a 'sixer' and two boundaries for 'fours'. The score was now 52 for us. Again I survived an over. Again Stan hit the Smardenites hip and thigh and the score came up to 62. I took Killick's bowling once more. We ran a single for a bye to give Stan the bowling 63. He hit a two to keep the ball: 65. Then he swung out for a boundary 'four', but failed, and we got three runs and our side was level at last. But I had the bowling and I could see the apprehension on Stan's hot and freckled face, his tousled curls gleaming in the sunlight. I saw Killick pale, grim and determined, walk back, turn and race up to the wicket. I never did see that ball he delivered, so I could not attempt to block it. Closing my eyes I just hit out where I hoped it would. Then I heard the glad sound of leather hitting willow and I opened my eyes to see the red ball speeding away to the 'four-run' boundary bordering the road beyond. 'Come on!' yelled Stan and away I galloped having scored the winning run! For that ball never reached the boundary, as it had been quickly and expertly fielded and slammed into the wicket-keeper, but by then Stan Turner, the real hero of that memorable game, had reached his crease.

******

Such a work as this could go on and on and on; for our adventures and experiences were as numberless as the sands upon the seashore.

Actually they began when my family came to live for a time, at the close of September 1919, with my grandparents at Pluckley until I left Mundy Bois some six years later for Chatham, the Blue Bell Hill country and the Dickens countryside of the Medway Towns, which I slowly grew to love – yet never so much, of course, as the village of my birth, Pluckley, from which I was absent for the best part of my childhood and tucked-away tiny Mundy Bois where I lived so happily and simply from December 1919 until one bright morning in April 1926. That is now just around thirty years ago. This work is my memorial to those wonderful days. This is not quite the end, for the last chapter is the next one, of the room where I dreamed my dreams and looked forward to the future.

*Pluckley was my playground*

*Lord, keep my memory green.*

*The Haunted Man*, the fifth of the Christmas books, by Charles Dickens

# CHAPTER EIGHTEEN

I always called it *my room*, though the back bedroom of our home at
Mundy Bois was shared with my brother Walter. Here I kept my
books, papers and periodicals. These were many and most varied. Piles
of the green-jacketed *Tit-Bits*, red-covered *Boys' Magazine*, *Nelson Lee*
libraries, *Union Jack* and *Aldines* 'Buffalo Bill' monthlies. In a box by the
bed I had my pressed wild flowers, fossils, wild birds' eggs and objects
found upon the seashore, at Hythe where my Aunt Annie lived, some
twenty miles away from our tiny hamlet. Then there was my collection
of cigarette cards comprising many useful sets: 'Historic Events',
'Coronation Series' (issued when King George V came to the throne),
'Overseas Dominions: Australia', 'Overseas Dominions: Canada',
'Victoria Cross', 'Great War' (1914-18) series, 'Animals and Birds of
Commercial Value', 'Plants of Commercial Value' and Wills'
wonderful set of 'British Birds' issued during 1917. There was also
Ogden's 'Boy Scout' series, all five of them: 'First Aid', 'Famous
Inventions', 'Regimental Uniforms', 'Fish and Bait', 'Old English
Garden Flowers' and 'Alpine Flowers'. My library of some seventy
volumes was very catholic in taste, ranging from Grimms' *Fairy Tales* to
*Last of the Mohicans*; *The Warlord of Mars* to *Tom Brown's Schooldays*;
*History of England* to *The Greyfriars Holiday Annual*; *Three in Norway* to
*Tales of Invention and Discovery*; *Michelin's Guide: Great Britain* to *Scouting
for Boys*; *The Peep of Day* to *Tit-Bits Football Annual* and *Tom Webster's
Daily Mail Sporting Cartoons*. I read everything I could get hold of: from
the Bible to the *Police News* – this surely does include everything!

This bedroom had scrubbed boards, with colour rush mats on each side of the bed and at the foot. Its walls were decorated with many photographs of famous sportsmen, football and cricket teams; coloured plates of an adventurous kind from the monthly magazine *The Boys' Own Paper* and nature photogravures from the fortnightly work *The Pageant of Nature*. A large coloured print showing all the birds migrating from Europe and Africa to the British Isles had pride of place on a wall near the top of the staircase. The window of this room looked out across the fields to Kingsland (Egerton) and the high-rising barrier of Lark Hill in the distance: to the right the green fields moved up to the base of the cliff-like Greenhill escarpment of Kentish ragstone: left were the flat fields to the line of Smarden Forest and beyond that the Weald of Kent. Each morning as I awoke from sleep meant a new day and fresh adventures: each morning, all the year round I would stand at the window for a few minutes and so see, very gradually unfolded, the seasons of the year. In this room, and in front of its window I dreamed my dreams, and found years later that I had not made them my master – yes, I loved Kipling's 'If' and almost everything he had ever written! My dreams I moulded to suit myself, time, and circumstances. For I came to write and to wander and explore. Came to know many very interesting people. Continuing always to learn, not alone from books, but also from mankind and Mother Nature.

THE END

# INDEX

# ABOUT THE AUTHOR

Frederick Sanders was born in Pluckley in 1908, but shortly afterwards moved with his family to various homes around the country. He returned to Pluckley in 1919 where he spent the next seven years, as described in *Pluckley was my Playground*. After an apprenticeship as a poultry farmer he moved to Chatham and helped to run the family shop in the town's High Street, before beginning a career at the dockyard. He wrote extensively on subjects relating to Kent: natural history, businesses, churchyards, dialect, and its ghosts and legends, on which he became a noted authority. He died in 1996.